Letters from a
Pastor's Heart

MATTHEW C. HARRISON

CONCORDIA PUBLISHING HOUSE · SAINT LOUIS

Published 2016 Concordia Publishing House
3558 S. Jefferson Ave., St. Louis, MO 63118-3968
1-800-325-3040 • www.cph.org

Some letters are taken from *The Lutheran Witness* articles featured in the "from the president" section, issues September 2010–April 2016.

Cover photo: © Kathy Harrison

All other photos: Erik M. Lunsford, © LCMS Communications

Manufactured in the United States of America

1 2 3 4 5 6 7 8 9 10   25 24 23 22 21 20 19 18 17 16

Contents

Introduction

Introduction

Twenty-five years ago, I was called to my first parish (town of 200, parish of 440 when I left). The day after receiving the call, while I was helping seminary professor Dr. Wally Degner paint his barn, I made a disparaging comment about the small-town people I was going to serve. Dr. Degner stopped dead in his tracks and wisely called me to account. I'll never forget his pastoral wisdom. "No, Matt . . . no, no. Don't do that! You are going to find that those people will be the most resourceful, hard-working, capable, and faithful people you will ever have the privilege of knowing." I was immediately humbled. Wow, was he right! That congregation was all of that and more. They took a young, inexperienced man, filled to the brim with book knowledge, and taught him how to be a pastor.

What did I learn?

A pastor is a shepherd. A shepherd has the heart of the "Good Shepherd." He loves his sheep. A shepherd leads by conviction, not coercion. Jesus exercised His authority by giving it up to death for His sheep (John 10:11). I soon learned that the whole point of the Lutheran Confessions (indeed, of the Bible itself) is comfort and consolation for dear Christian souls by means of the Gospel of free forgiveness.

For, as the apostle testifies:

> Whatever was written in former days was written for our instruction, that through endurance and through the encouragement of the Scriptures we might have hope. (Romans 15:4)

> But when this consolation and hope are weakened or entirely removed by Scripture, it is certain that it is understood and explained contrary to the Holy Spirit's will and meaning. (FC SD XI 92)

I learned to preach by studying the text of the Scriptures to be sure, but I also learned by spending time with the flock. Every spring, I meet with graduating seminarians and their wives here in St. Louis. They are wonderful young men, eager to set out on their life's calling to serve Christ. I always tell them that they are entering what has to be the most amazing vocation on earth. Their people will invite them into their most troubled, embarrassing, and painful life situations. Like I have, these young men will carry on vigils at deathbed after deathbed. And wonder of wonders, those same folks will invite them into their most joyous and happy situations—Baptisms, confirmations, weddings, graduations, anniversaries, and much more. They will actually be used by God to lead people to know Jesus (2 Timothy 4:5). There simply is no greater honor (1 Timothy 5:17).

In that small community, I learned that a pastor wears out his shoes. I wore out cowboy boots in those early years—visiting every farm, every home, every business; driving mile after mile for hospital calls. Later, serving a parish in the poorest census track in Indiana, I went through pair after pair of leather-soled shoes. That allowed me to witness of Christ to the cobbler! A fellow pastor gave me great advice. "If you have the feeling that you need to speak to someone in your congregation, don't wait. Do it." I visited virtually every nonmember home in the area to share Christ and invite people to church. On one occasion, I knocked on the door of a farmhouse. I quickly found out I'd come upon the home of a family of Jehovah's Witnesses. "Well," I said to the father, "isn't this a turn of events?" When I let out a belly laugh, he couldn't help but join me. Then he heard the true Gospel.

I also learned to appreciate the truth of the royal priesthood (1 Peter 2:9–10). I watched in awe as marvelous laypeople witnessed of Christ to their friends, family, and neighbors, often in very extraordinary and persistent ways. I learned that God provides competent laypeople to serve on the board of elders and in all the offices at church. In the parishes where I have served, there have been people with remarkable abilities, financial and business acumen, and just plain down-to-earth know-how. They kept the congregation on the right course, financially and otherwise. They loved their Lord. They loved their church. They loved being Lutherans. And wonder of wonders, they loved their pastor. "Pastor, you take care of the flock. We'll make sure this place is well taken care of and shipshape for the mission."

I learned that whenever I made a decision in an emotionally charged context, I virtually always made the wrong decision (Proverbs 2:1–11). Wow, do things always look different after a night's rest! But as I made mistakes, I learned to apologize quickly and ask for forgiveness. I did make mistakes (and still do). I marveled at my people's willingness to forgive me. I became convinced that pastoral leadership means leading also in repentance (1 Timothy 1:15).

I tell seminarians that there are two ways to get into trouble quickly: (1) make changes immediately; and (2) fail to visit the flock. A young pastor, filled to the brim with solid doctrine and ideas of correct practice, faces a challenge. How will he react when things are not what he's been taught or is convinced they should be in a Lutheran parish? The temptation is to fail to consult with others, fail to begin and continue the steady process of teaching, and instead to make quick unilateral decisions. I think young pastors often fear that if they don't make immediate improvements, they may over time devolve into a state of complacency and complicity with less than good theology and practice. In my case, I read the Bible and also translated the works of the great Lutheran historian Hermann Sasse. I came to realize that the church has a long history. Congregations have very long histories too. A pastorate may well be of short duration by comparison. The art of pastoring a congregation means being able to live "on the rough edge," while having an idea of the goal ahead and patiently working toward that goal. It means teaching, teaching, and more teaching (2 Timothy 2:24). Our solid, biblical, and confessionally Lutheran teaching is our greatest asset. It's all about solid Law and Gospel, solid teaching for life and life eternal (2 Timothy 2:15). One must teach and allow God's Word to work in the lives of people (Matthew 13:8).

In a church body that has a history of polarization, I simply refused to allow strong Lutheran doctrine to be pitted against mission to the lost (Luke 19:10). In every ministry I've ever served, I've had someone telling me, "You can't hold to the letter of the Lutheran Confessions and do real ministry." I respond, "You not only can, but you must." The official teachings of the Lutheran Church are a treasure. They set forth the truth of the Gospel and the inerrant Word of God. Lutheran churches and other Christians from all over the world are flocking to us because of it. Lutheran churches that fail to hold solidly to this standard always go the way of the flesh. And it's my deepest conviction that when we hold to our Bible, Small Catechism, and Book of Concord, these documents provide the greatest strength and encouragement to engage the world. Just feast your mind's eye on this fabulous quotation from Luther on faith, taken from our Book of Concord:

> Faith must be the mother and source of works
> that are truly good and well pleasing to God,
> which God will reward in this world and in

the world to come. This is why St. Paul calls them true fruit of faith, also fruit of the Spirit [Galatians 5:22–23]. For, as Dr. Luther writes in the Preface to St. Paul's Epistle to the Romans:

Faith, however, is a divine work in us that changes us and makes us to be born anew of God, John 1[:12–13]. It kills the old Adam and makes us altogether different men, in heart and spirit and mind and powers; it brings with it the Holy Spirit. O, it is a living, busy, active, mighty thing, this faith. It is impossible for it not to be doing good works incessantly. It does not ask whether good works are to be done, but before the question is asked, it has already done them, and is constantly doing them. Whoever does not do such works, however, is an unbeliever. He gropes and looks around for faith and good works, but knows neither what faith is nor what good works are. Yet he talks and talks, with many words, about faith and good works.

Faith is a living, daring confidence in God's grace, so sure and certain that the believer would stake his life on it a thousand times. This knowledge of and confidence in God's grace makes men glad and bold and happy in dealing with God and all creatures. And this is the work that the Holy Spirit performs in faith. Because of it, without compulsion, a person is ready and glad to do good to everyone, to serve everyone, to suffer everything, out of love and praise to God, who has shown him this grace. Thus it is impossible to separate works from faith, quite as impossible as to separate heat and light from fire. [LW 35:370–71] (FC SD IV 9–12)

In that small parish, I learned just how vital it is to know the community and find points of contact (1 Corinthians 9:22). Every community has its points of pride. Participating in the community is a potentially strong affirmation of the good things going on in the "left-hand kingdom," where it is not only possible but also often very wise to work together for good, civil ends. That conviction served me well in the city parish I served later.

I also believe deeply in honesty (1 Timothy 3:2). I've been accused of "wearing my heart on my sleeve." I love taking questions from the floor, off the cuff, at district conventions and other events. And I learned long ago, if you say what you actually believe to be true, your story will *always* be the same (Ephesians 4:15). In the church, we have deep convictions and concerns. That's why it is always important for pastors to deal with others with kindness, patience, and forgiveness (Colossians 3:12–17).

My decade leading the national Synod's mercy and disaster work only reenforced these fundamental convictions. The church has a corporate life of mercy, especially to those in its midst, but also beyond (Luke 6:36; Galatians 6:10; 2 Corinthians 8–9). I was convinced that if we set forth a solid, biblical, and Lutheran reason for caring for the neighbor in body and soul, if we showed the church—even those parts of the church that had not shown a great deal of interest in human care—that Jesus, St. Paul, Luther, C. F. W. Walther, and all the fathers and mothers of the church were proponents of the church's corporate life of mercy, people would rally to engage. That happened, as we did our part. I've been amazed at what God has continued to do through the people of the Missouri Synod.

Not long after being elected in 2010, I was visiting the home of Jobst Schoene, the Bishop Emeritus of our German partner church. He has a study in his home, and there stands his prayer kneeler. The candles are burned to nubs; the indentations on the kneeling pad from his knees are deeply worn. The pages of his Bible, open to the Psalms, are virtually transparent from the oil of his hands. It cut me to the heart. I need to learn to pray, I thought to myself. Soon I built a kneeler for my office. Every day, it beckons me first thing, and I fall to my knees in prayer. From the start, I began writing down those people and institutions, churches, pastors, congregations, and families for whom I pray almost daily. The amazing thing is that I have on that kneeler all the notes written over these years. And more amazing is the fact that those notes now remind me of prayer after prayer answered. Jesus prayed often (Matthew 14:13). Jesus invites us to pray for ourselves and the mission of the Church (Matthew 6:9–15; 9:38). The apostle Paul writes, "Pray without ceasing" (1 Thessalonians 5:17). And I am never so thankful as when I hear that someone or some congregation is praying for me.

As I've written these pastoral letters over the years as president, these are the fundamentals that have remained constant. It has been my deepest goal and desire that the LCMS be ever more a community united in doctrine and mission. And the Lord has blessed remarkably over the history of the Synod and in these last years.

It has been my deep honor to serve. In the Lord's time, I shall shuffle off to obscurity as the Synod in its wisdom chooses the next man, under divine grace and guidance, to serve as president. And I shall be happy to do so when that time comes. Finally, I'm just not that significant in the grand scheme of things. Let us work while it is day (John 9:4)!

I want to thank Village Lutheran Church, where I serve as a called assistant pastor. The job of president requires my absence all too often, but serving as I can and do under Rev. Dr. Kevin Golden is a blessing and joy for me. I also want to thank Adriane Heins for her able service as editor of our marvelous *The Lutheran Witness*, where most of these letters were first published. I thank Dr. Bruce Kintz and the staff at CPH for their consummate dedication to the mission of Christ. I thank my staff and especially Rev. Drs. Herb Mueller and Jon Vieker, for their gift of attention to detail and good counsel. And I give thanks to my lovely and gracious soul mate, Kathy, and my two sons, Matthew and Mark, the joy of our lives. We suffered a house fire this past summer, and what has followed has been the most difficult year of our lives. Yet, it has been the most blessed too (Philippians 4:12).

Finally, some few years ago, my parents were wintering in Florida. When the pastor there learned that my parents were in the congregation that Sunday, he introduced them after church. As they were leaving, a woman came up to my mother and said, "I want you to know that this church prays for your son every Sunday." Just as my mother was choking back her motherly pride and feigning a bit of humility in thanking her, the woman continued, "Is there some problem?" Ha! There is no problem, but there is the Missouri Synod, which can be a bit challenging at times!

Which reminds me, a pastor prays. I pray for you. And I covet your prayers.

Pastor Matthew C. Harrison
Easter 2016

Repentance

Beginning with Repentance

The greatest eras in the history of the Church have all begun with repentance. Those times when the Gospel of free forgiveness by faith in Jesus Christ has shone brightest in missionary witness and expansion—in a burning desire to care for the weak and needy with Christ's own mercy, and in zealous and creative endeavors in church life and organization—have all begun with the preaching of repentance.

It's hardly a coincidence that John the Baptizer's first recorded words were "Repent, for the kingdom of heaven is at hand!" (Matthew 3:2). It's no accident that the first words out of Jesus' mouth when He began His public ministry were likewise, "Repent, for the kingdom of heaven is at hand!" (Matthew 4:17). And note that the text says, "from that time [forward] Jesus began to preach" repentance. *Jesus, the greatest preacher ever, was throughout His ministry a preacher of repentance.* After Jesus' death and resurrection—the grand payment and absolution for all the sins of the world, past, present and future—Peter repented and was restored following his own miserable defection and denial. And then Peter and the rest of the apostles burst upon the world with a glorious preaching of repentance. At Pentecost, Peter preached the thunder of the Law: "'This Jesus whom you crucified, God has made both Lord and Christ.' Now when they heard this they were cut to the heart, and said to Peter and the rest of the apostles, 'Brothers, what shall we do?' Peter responded with the sweet comfort of the Gospel: 'Repent and be baptized every one of you in the name of Jesus Christ for the forgiveness of your sins'" (Acts 2:36–38).

The Reformation began the same way. The very first words of Luther's Ninety-Five Theses declare: "When our Lord and Master Jesus Christ says 'Repent,' he wills that the entire life of the Christian be one of repentance." *The Reformation began with a divine call to repentance*—with a confession of sin and a rejection of the delusion that human activity can in any way, whole or in part, bring about salvation or divine favor.

Why have we lacked missionary zeal? Why have we been so divided? Why have we failed to love each other? Why have we struggled financially? Why have we failed to convince both those within and outside our fellowship? Why have we been unable to listen to our brothers and sisters? Why has our preaching so often lacked urgency and biblical depth? Are we preachers therapists, or are we prophets of God with a clear message of Law and Gospel? Are we still the Church that preaches Jesus' own message of repentance? As I write these things, I am thinking above all of myself, of my own sins.

There is nothing for any of us in the Missouri Synod to be smug about. "For what do you have that you have not been given?" Luther reminded the Germans of his day that the precious Gospel can be and has, in fact, been lost by whole nations.

> Buy while the market is at your door; gather in the harvest while there is sunshine and fair weather; make use of God's grace and word while it is there! *For you should know that God's word and grace is like a passing shower of rain which does not return where it has once been . . . when it's gone it's gone. . . .* And you Germans need not think that you will have it forever, for ingratitude and contempt will not make it stay. Therefore, seize it and hold it fast. (Luther's Works 45:352)

The good news is that the Lord delights in having mercy upon sinners, just like us. In fact, "Christ dwells only in sinners" (Luther). That means that Christ dwells only in a Church made up of sinners—people and pastors just like us. If we won't be sinners (Repent!), we shall have no Savior.

Jesus has given us an astounding gift. We have the treasure of the Gospel so marvelously and biblically laid before us by Luther's Small Catechism. May the Lord grant us repentance, all of us, that the Gospel not pass from us and that we poor sinners—yes, the Missouri Synod—might be His own tool to preach repentance, forgiveness and faith in His name—even now, even today.

The Missouri Synod Needs Advent

What is the single most critical issue in the life of the Missouri Synod? Is it evangelism? Church planting? Missions? Seminaries? Church-worker well-being? Theology? Congregational vitality? Finances? Education? Mercy?

I submit to you, dear reader, that the single most vital issue facing this church body today is our great need for individual and collective *repentance*—thoroughgoing sorrow over sin and faith that grabs hold of the Savior of sinners, Jesus. The Missouri Synod needs Advent.

Advent is a matter of repentance. Repentance is a matter of eternal life and death. "Prepare the way of the Lord; make his paths straight!" (Matthew 3:3). Advent is about sinners recognizing themselves as sinners in the face of the coming Lord. The eternal Lord of the universe came as a babe at Bethlehem. He comes in His Word and Sacrament. He shall come again in the end. If you meet Him secure in your sins, whether at the Communion rail or on the Last Day, you shall die in your sins, eternally.

Just a month ago we celebrated the Reformation. There was a great deal of huffing and puffing about our heritage. But we miss the whole point of Luther and the Reformation if we fail to recognize that it was all about repentance. In 1817, Klaus Harms famously said about his times: "Before the Reformation, the forgiveness of sins at least cost something. Now it's completely free, and everyone freely rewards themselves with it." That statement perfectly depicts our times too. But worse, it also sadly depicts our church in large measure. The Missouri Synod needs repentance. The Missouri Synod needs—as a matter of her life and death—the first word out of John the Baptizer's mouth: "Repent!" (Matthew 3:2).

So much of our preaching lacks the textual fire and energy of our evangelical birthright! So often our laity have an inclination that preaching could be better but have no idea what Lutheran preaching should be. Pastors and people, repent! And bear the fruit of repentance! Read, mark and inwardly digest C. F. W. Walther's *The Proper Distinction between Law and Gospel*.

Yes, your pastor could be doing a better job of preaching and visiting (he needs to repent, be forgiven and encouraged by grace), but you allow unhealthy and unchristian gossip and even take part in it yourself! Perhaps you are in a congregation with generations of unhealthy behavior! This is no joke! The Lord does not leave unpunished the despising of His Word. Repent! The wages of sin is death, but the free gift of God is eternal life in Jesus Christ, our Lord!

Pastors! You head off half-cocked and do whatever you wish without regard to its effects upon your brother pastors and sister congregations. Some of you elicit little or no concern for the unchurched people who pass by your building daily. You grumble about each other and do everything but sit down and humbly resolve the issues, failing to realize that love not only covers a multitude of sins (1 Peter 4:8) but also entails curtailing one's own freedom in order not to offend (Romans 14). Repent! This is the kind of sin of thanklessness that causes the Lord to move His Gospel, like a passing rain shower, away from us to others (Luther's Works, vol. 45, p. 352; see also *At Home in the House of My Fathers*, CPH, 2011, pp. 776ff.).

Friends, I may know a couple of your sins, but I know many, many more of my own. Under the Law, I, too, am nothing but a damned sinner. My prayer life wavers. I'm not what I should be as a father and husband. My love for God's Word is often grown cold. I worry. "Wretched man that I am! Who will deliver me from this body of death?" (Romans 7:24).

Grant repentance, O Lord!

Grant faith, O Lord!

Grant forgiveness, O Lord!

Grant us love for each other, O Lord!

Grant us zeal for the Gospel and those who need it,
    O Lord!

Renew our preaching and our hearing, O Lord!

O Lord, grant us Your Advent!

Come quickly, and save us!

Forgiveness

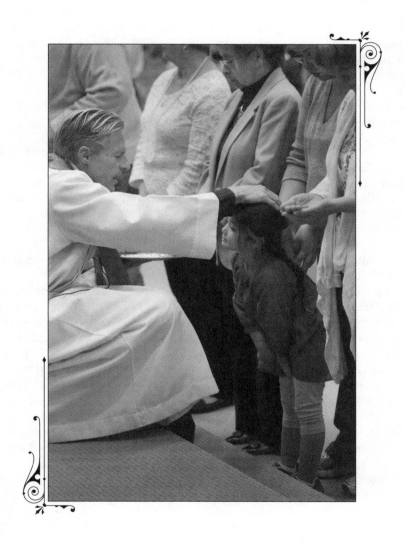

The Joy of Forgiveness

I *didn't come to kill you."* He was an imposing figure. He had an even more imposing reputation. But what he had been known for, well-earned to be sure, was not why I remember him. He had become an ever more devout Missouri Synod Lutheran and regularly shared the good news of Jesus with, and invited to church, people who wouldn't have given him the time of day had he not been who he had been. This former purveyor of intimidation had become an ambassador of reconciliation. This fact was all the more significant because it was not readily apparent. He was so unassuming, even with his rather imposing stature, that no one who hadn't come to know him would be aware of his past. Same man, same haunts, same circle of people—but for an ever-deepening, transformative joy of being justified in Christ.

Another man in a nearby community had sinned egregiously against my friend and his family. The former "intimidator" went directly to the man in question, to his very doorstep in fact. The guilty party opened the door and began frantically to plead (with good reason), "Don't kill me! Don't kill me!" My friend responded, "I didn't come to kill you. I came to forgive you." He wasn't on a mission of retribution. He was on a mission of reconciliation. *"If your neighbor sins against you, go and tell him his fault, between you and him alone"* (Matthew 18:15). He hadn't come to exact justice. He had come as one justified sinner seeking the repentance of and reconciliation with another sinner. The flesh relishes the thought of retribution. The spirit rejoices in reconciliation.

The righteousness of Christ credited by faith is transformative. It reckons us what we are not and cannot be in and of ourselves—perfectly righteous with the righteousness of Jesus. We are reckoned "just." Then, like a good tree planted, it produces more and more fruit (Matthew 7:17), especially joy, and makes us evermore what we have been freely declared to be—righteous in Christ. Declared forgiven, we cannot but be forgiving. But let's back up.

St. Paul says that this righteousness was obtained fully by Christ's cross—*"we have now been justified by his blood."* What has been achieved, obtained, and perfected by Christ outside of us, before us, and without us (two thousand years ago on a cross and via a resurrection), is delivered to us and reckoned to us in the word of the Gospel. Because it's already accomplished, it can't be achieved by doing anything. The deed is done. That's why Jesus' last words were "It is finished" (John 19:30). The benefits of Christ's death and resurrection are received, laid hold of, by faith. Faith simply lays hold of the gift, and even the faith, which receives the gift, is itself all gift. So St. Paul wrote, *"For by grace you have been saved through faith. And this is not your own doing; it is the gift of God, not a result of works, so that no one may boast"* (Ephesians 2:8–9). . . . When we confront God, He says to us, "I didn't come to kill you. I came to forgive you." *"For God did not send his Son into the world to condemn the world, but in order that the world might be saved through him"* (John 3:17). Equipped with such joy . . . we find ourselves freed to act as God Himself with our neighbor. "I didn't come to kill you. I came to forgive you." Joy! *"We also rejoice in God through our Lord Jesus Christ, through whom we have now received reconciliation"* (Romans 5:11).

—(Excerpted from *A Little Book on Joy* [CPH, 2011], pp. 44–47.)

Justification, Our "Chief Article"

"This article concerning justification by faith . . . is the chief article in the entire Christian doctrine, without which no poor conscience can have any firm consolation, or can truly know the riches of the grace of Christ." (FC SD III 6)

It's not uncommon to hear it said that the word *justification* ought not be used. Our Lutheran Confessions, however, call it the "chief article." Actually, there is nothing more familiar to people today than "justification." Not only are we the most litigious society in history, all of us are bent on self-justification. I justify my actions; my production at work; my inaction. I justify my failings; my claims to respect; my "people." I justify my feelings of anger or hatred; my attitudes. I justify myself over against my family, colleagues, etc. It never ends. Self-justification is often the bane of our existence, particularly in relationships in home, family and church. With God, self-justification is deadly.

God's response to our self-justification over against Him is very simple. "Now we know that whatever the law says it speaks to those who are under the law, so that every mouth may be stopped, and the whole world held accountable to God. For by works of the law no human being will be justified in his sight" (Romans 3:19f.). The Reformation breakthrough of Luther was about justification. Luther realized that the Bible speaks of justification in two distinct ways. The Law says, "Do this and you will live" (Luke 10:29). This kind of "active righteousness," however, terrified Luther because he knew that he was a sinner. Jesus wants more than just hands, feet and mouth. He demands that the heart and mind be sinless (Matthew 5:17). Trying to accomplish that leads only to self-deception and arrogance or despair (e.g., the Pharisee and the tax collector; Luke 18:9–13).

Luther was studying Romans 1:16–17: "I am not ashamed of the Gospel, for it is the power of God for salvation for everyone who believes. . . . 'The righteous shall live by faith.'" Suddenly, Luther realized it was not about an active righteousness (our actions), but about a passive righteousness (God's actions in Christ credited to us freely)! The righteous requirements of the Law were fulfilled by Christ's perfect life and death, to pay for our sins! The result? Righteousness—a "not guilty" verdict, rendered upon mankind in Christ, and appropriated by faith alone. (Read Romans 3–4.) This has many ramifications.

1. Everything that Christ is and does is declared ("imputed") to be ours! He gets our death, sin and hell. We get His life, death and resurrection credited to our account. "He who knew no sin became sin for us that we might become the righteousness of God" (2 Corinthians 5:21; cf. Romans 4:6; Philippians 3:9; Jeremiah 23:5f.).

2. This "righteousness" is delivered to us by means of the Gospel (Romans 1:16).

3. This "righteousness" is delivered by Holy Absolution, whether privately by a Christian or publicly by our pastor. "Whosoever sins you forgive . . ." (Matthew 16:19; 18:15ff.; John 20:22f.).

4. This "righteousness" is delivered by Holy Baptism. "For as many of you as were baptized into Christ have put on Christ" (Galatians 3:27; Isaiah 61:10). "He saved us, not because of works done by us in righteousness (active), but according to his own mercy, by the washing of regeneration and renewal of the Holy Spirit, whom he poured out on us richly . . . so that being justified (passive) by his grace," etc. (Titus 3:5–6).

5. It's delivered by the Lord's Supper. "Take and eat . . . for the forgiveness of your sins."

6. This delivery depends upon God's mercy, not our work. It is received by faith only. The deed was finished almost 2,000 years ago. "God was in Christ reconciling the world to himself" (2 Corinthians 5:19). Faith merely grabs hold of Christ. "Abraham believed God, and it was credited to him as righteousness" (Romans 4:3; Galatians 3:6f.).

7. Because justification is totally Christ's act, it is absolutely certain. "There is now no condemnation for those who are in Christ Jesus" (Romans 8:1).

8. We are completely sure of God's attitude toward us. "Since we have been justified by faith, we have peace with God through our Lord Jesus Christ" (Romans 5:1).

9. Our righteousness in Christ is certain. So we have a solid sure hope. "Through him we have obtained access by faith into this grace in which we stand, and we rejoice in hope of the glory of God" (Romans 5:2).

10. We can even rejoice when we suffer. God is not against us. In fact, "all things work together for good for those called . . ." (Romans 8:28; 5:3–4).

11. We are declared just, and freed to live with gusto. "For freedom Christ has set us free!" (Galatians 5:1; Romans 14:17). We are freed not to expect those around us to be without sin! (Galatians 2:17; Romans 3:22f.). We are forgiven. We forgive! (Matthew 18:15ff., 33).

This is all worth confessing—both for our own sake and for the sake of others. "For with the heart one believes and is justified, and with the mouth one confesses and is saved" (Romans 10:9–10).

Regarded by God . . . and Others

I thank God and Jesus Christ that someone has regarded us as human beings." I've never heard anything so profound, and this from the lips of a young boy in Kenya. LCMS World Relief and Human Care had built an orphanage where he and his fellow AIDS orphans were now to be cared for. Amidst the tears, his word *regarded* caught my attention.

Regarded is at the heart of the Lutheran Confession of the faith, as confessed in the Augsburg Confession, Article IV on justification. It is the door to eternity. And it is also the most powerful, freeing, compelling force for a joyous life in God's mercy, driving us to act mercifully to our neighbor in need. In Christ, God "regards" us as human beings.

> Our churches also teach that men cannot be justified before God by their own strength, merits, or works but are freely justified for Christ's sake through faith when they believe that they are received into favor and that their sins are forgiven on account of Christ, who by his death made satisfaction for our sins. This faith God imputes [i.e., regards, reckons] for righteousness in his sight. (Romans 3–4)

Note that little word *impute*. In the Gospel, God *imputes*, *reckons*, *regards*, *credits*, *accounts* faith in Jesus as righteousness. "For by grace you have been saved through faith. And this is not your doing; it is the gift of God" (Ephesians 2:8). Thus, I am *reckoned*, justified, sinless, not guilty on account of Jesus. Faith merely grabs hold of Jesus. The good boasting in the Bible is about Jesus (Galatians 6:14)! In Jesus, God recognizes me as somebody. In fact, "God was in Christ reconciling the world to himself, not counting their trespasses against them" (2 Corinthians 5:19). There is not a living soul in this world who is not worth the very blood of Jesus. God accounts each individual as just that precious.

Is this justification stuff all ethereal mumbo-jumbo having nothing to do with real life? Not so. Oswald Bayer points out that justification is fundamental to all human existence.

There is no such thing as an autocratic individual, totally independent of the surrounding
world and its recognition. . . . Striving to find
approval in the eyes of others, being noticed
and not being dismissed as nothing by others,
demonstrates that I cannot relate to myself without relating to the world. It applies to our social
birth as well as our physical birth. I constantly
vacillate even to the very end of life, between
the judgment others make about me and my own
judgment of myself. . . . I arrive at some point of
calm, and then become unsure of myself again.
(*Living by Faith: Justification and Sanctification*
[Eerdmans, 2003], p. 3)

God's solution for our sin, and for our deepest need in time
and eternity, has been to *regard* us as valuable as "His holy precious blood and His innocent suffering and death." And this frees
us to *regard* those around us in the same—to acknowledge, to
recognize, to value, to listen, to forgive, to have compassion, to
speak up for, to act in mercy. Then we shall soon find them saying, "I thank God and Jesus Christ that you have regarded me as
a human being."

Back to Basics: Law and Gospel

A t the heart of virtually every problem in the church, at the bottom of every strained relationship, at the center of every reason an inactive member stays home on Sunday or leaves the LCMS is the issue of the proper distinguishing between the Law and the Gospel. Without this understanding, the Scriptures make no sense, we will have no idea why we go to church (or worse, the wrong idea) and we will have no clue as to why orthodox Lutheranism reflects New Testament Christianity in the best sense. We may well be a royal pain and terror to those around us. Even worse, without a clear understanding of Law and Gospel, we'll be of no use to people around us struggling with spiritual and life issues. Worse still, we may even become a millstone round their necks, helping them (and ourselves) on the way to hell!

The Lutheran Reformation began when the Lord God Himself, through the Scriptures, opened Luther's mind to the scriptural distinction between the Law and the Gospel. The Law makes demands, which we could not, cannot and never will fulfill. "No one is righteous, no not one" (Romans 3:10). "Even our righteous deeds are as filthy rags" (Isaiah 64:6). "The wages of sin is death" (Romans 6:23). If St. Paul laments about himself, "The good that I would do I do not do" (Romans 7:19), where does that leave you? You have not a thought, an action or any of your physical, psychological or spiritual being that is not affected by and tainted by the reality of sin. And sin damns.

The Gospel, however, makes no demands and even gives the faith needed to believe it (Ephesians 2:8–9). The Gospel is the forgiveness of sins. Christ was slain from the foundation of the world for you (Matthew 25:34). Christ was prophesied in the Old Testament for you (Isaiah 53). Christ was conceived for you (Luke 1:26). Christ was born for you (Luke 2). Christ was circumcised and fulfilled the Old Testament ceremonial law for you (Luke 2:22). The boy Christ taught in the temple for you! (You get the credit for His diligence in the catechism! See Luke 2:41.) John the Baptizer pointed to Jesus, saying, "Behold, the Lamb of God, who takes away the sin of the world!" (John 1:29)—for you. Jesus was baptized for you (Luke 3:21). Jesus was tempted for you (Luke 4). All of Jesus' miracles, healings, words, promises, His Passion, His trials, His beating, His betrayal, His crucifixion, His ridicule, His words on the cross—"Forgive them, Lord, for they know not what they do!" (Luke 23:34); "Today you will be with me in paradise!" (Luke 23:43)—His death, His descent in victory to hell and His glorious resurrection and ascension are all, all of it, for you! And that's all Gospel!

But there is even better news, and this is the point where the devil bedevils us. What Jesus attained for us some 6,000 miles away and 2,000 years ago is delivered in the word of preaching, in Baptism, in absolution and in the Supper. "I don't need to go to church to be a Christian." Oh, yeah? God says you do. "Do not give up meeting together." (See all of Hebrews 10.) But better than the Law (which says you should go to church) is the blessed Gospel! We cry like the tax collector at church, "God, be merciful to me, a sinner!" (Luke 18:13). And the pastor says, "In the stead and by the command of Christ, forgiven!" (see John 20:21–23). He makes the sign of the cross to remind us that we're baptized, forgiven (Titus 3:5). The Scriptures are read, and they contain both Law (demand, threat) and Gospel (forgiveness, promise). The sermon is preached, and the texts explained. The Law threatens and drives us to Jesus! The Gospel is not merely described or spoken about, it's delivered! "The gospel is the power of God unto salvation" (Romans 1:16), right now, for you!

Most people who stop going to church or get church wrong think it's about ethics. They think it's about following the rules (i.e., following the Law). No, it's finally about sinners receiving forgiveness (Gospel). And blessed by the Benediction ("The Lord bless you and keep you! The Lord make His face shine upon you and be gracious to you"—Gospel!) and all the forgiveness given, forgiven sinners head back into their vocations in life to be a beautiful leaven. If I know I'm a real "hard-boiled sinner" who's been forgiven (Luther), I cannot be an unforgiving jackass to those around me. It's a matter of Law and Gospel. I cannot but speak forgiveness—the Lord's own forgiveness—to others.

Jesus Welcomes Sinners

A recent television documentary covered the famous "Woodstock" concert in New York State. I grew up with the music and did and do enjoy much of it. I was seven years old in 1969 and, aside from seeing the Vietnam casualty reports on the evening news, I was blissfully unaware of the unraveling of American culture.

The documentary, all filmed at the three-day concert, struck me profoundly. The normality of the young people interviewed, the pervasiveness of drugs, the undertone of sexual experimentation, the understandable disillusionment with war and the rejection of standard political solutions were all tremendous portents of the cultural tsunami we are now experiencing. And based on the size of the crowd, make no mistake, there were thousands of LCMS youth there too.

Much of the countercultural agenda articulated in 1969 has been achieved in the years since. Artists who performed in that muddy field in upstate New York are passing from this world, while those living singers, now in their 70s (like Joan Baez) and older, have become radical champions of our cultural implosion today. Their goal was peace and love. Seeing the likes of a young Jerry Garcia of "The Grateful Dead" joke about marijuana stunned me as I contemplated his life, marked by struggling with a drug addiction that finally killed him. Watching Jimi Hendrix, who would be dead of an overdose just 13 months later, filled me with even more melancholy. Man seeks freedom by his own devices, only to become enslaved.

We live today with a "Purple Haze" of confusion over many issues, and no issue more so than sexuality. Our job as the church is not to Christianize our society. Not at all. We do our best as pastors and teachers and church to teach what the Bible says about church and state, about natural law, morality and marriage, and we encourage you to be active in your communities, politically and otherwise. It *is* our task to teach to those in the Church what the Bible says about marriage and sex. We have done this, and much of it has been done very well. But it is past time for us to up our game in this regard. We have the herculean task of teaching our people what God in Christ expects of us in the realm of marriage, family and sexuality. The pressures of our culture toward the acceptance of the gay agenda, and the secular sexual agenda *in toto*, are pressures upon us. And they are ever increasing.

Some time ago we resolved to begin working more intentionally in the area of caring for those who struggle with same-sex attraction. We assembled a group of individuals, each with significant experience in this area, and we asked them: "Where do we go?" "What do we do as the Church?" The weekly preaching that our pastors do—condemning us sinners and delivering the forgiveness of sins—is pure gold. It's the *sine qua non* of dealing with the Sixth Commandment sins of thought, word and deed with which we all struggle. But we also assembled the "God's Gift of Sexuality" task force on same-sex attraction, believing that it was time for the Synod to begin to identify existing LCMS capacity and knowledge on this issue.

Several years ago, we took this approach in the area of disaster ministry. The result was an overwhelming strengthening and networking and use of unending capacity within our own church body to care for people in times of disaster. We can do the same with same-sex attraction. It's time to recognize, increase and share our resources to reach out to individuals and families who are struggling with these issues so we can share their burdens. Even though the Bible prevents us from affirming same-sex marriage and same-sex attraction, we must nevertheless be welcoming to those who struggle. We are all sinners. Jesus welcomes sinners. Jesus came to have mercy upon us sinners, and He does.

The Bible

How Does Jesus View the Bible?

The US Department of Justice has made it clear that in cases where religious freedom comes into conflict with sexual freedom (particularly same-sex relationships, but we saw this principle at work also in the Health and Human Services regulations on insurance companies providing *abortifacients*), the government will advocate for sexual freedom. This is ironic since the First Amendment specifically guarantees the free exercise of religion. With culture in full transformation about us, the sexual revolution long behind us, how do we maintain our Christian bearings? This question is acute, particularly for young people on college campuses where "diversity" is celebrated—usually as long as this does not include acceptance of historic Christianity.

Critics of our belief in the divinely inspired Scriptures (2 Peter 1:21) have often asserted that our alleged infantile faith has been duped into believing in a perfect, divine book that plopped down somehow from heaven and then doing, in a ridiculous and wooden fashion, everything that the book demands. That just isn't so.

Faith is God's precious gift (Ephesians 2:8–9). It is worked by Him (Romans 1:16). The object of faith is Christ (John 14:6–7; John 3:16). Faith is worked by God's own instruments: the proclaimed (or read) Word of forgiveness in the death and resurrection of Jesus (1 Corinthians 3:5; 4:15; 15:1–2), Baptism (Acts 2:41; John 3:5; Acts 22:16) and the Lord's Supper (Matthew 26:26–27). Condemned and convicted by the Law (Romans 3:19), we are converted by the Word of the Gospel, indeed, "the righteousness of God through faith in Jesus Christ for all who believe. For there is no distinction: for all have sinned and fall short of the glory of God, and are justified by his grace as a gift, through the redemption that is in Christ Jesus" (Romans 3:22–24).

Believing solely in Jesus for forgiveness, we cry out to Jesus like Peter, "Lord, to whom shall we go? You have the words of eternal life!" (John 6:68). Jesus directs us to His very *words* for truth (John 8:32). And Jesus teaches us plenty about Himself—Law, Gospel, repentance, forgiveness, Baptism, Lord's Supper, absolution and yes, sexuality (and much, much more). Jesus also teaches us about the Bible. Once we believe in Jesus—the very Son of God, God in the flesh—we are interested not only in what He actually said and did, but also especially in how *He* views the Scriptures!

For Jesus, the words of the Bible are true assertions, readily applicable to life. Jesus says the whole Bible points to Him. "They . . . bear witness about me" (John 5:39)! "It is written," He stated three times in the face of the devil's temptations (Matthew 4). For Jesus, the Bible is absolutely authoritative and a sword to be wielded against temptations and attacks. Jesus did not set aside the Bible. He fulfilled the Old Testament (Matthew 5:17ff.) and intensified the moral law (Matthew 5:21ff.)! As He used the Bible to teach, He believed that the people and events spoken of in the Old Testament were real—like Solomon (Matthew 6:29), Jonah and the big fish (Matthew 16:4; 12:38ff.), Adam and Eve (Matthew 19:3ff.), Moses (Matthew 8:4), David (Matthew 12:3) and Abraham, Isaac and Jacob (Matthew 8:11). Jesus believed that the Old Testament contained prophecies that were and are fulfilled (Luke 4:21; Matthew 11:1–10; 13:10–17), that the Bible did not have errors (John 10:35) and that the Holy Spirit prompted the Old Testament writers (Mark 12:36). Finally, He confessed that the Old Testament Scriptures prophesied His suffering and resurrection, and He promised that the Holy Spirit would be given to His apostles as they bore witness to Him (Luke 24:44; John 14:22ff.), which they did, particularly in writing the New Testament (John 14:26). Thus, we have the authoritative New Testament, which is likewise the very Word of God.

Paul's view is none other than Jesus' own view when he writes, "All Scripture is given by inspiration of God, and is profitable for doctrine, for reproof, for correction, for instruction in righteousness" (2 Timothy 3:16 NKJV). We believe the Bible because we know our Shepherd, and we recognize His voice in the Scriptures (John 10:27).

It's very safe and chic these days to say, "I'm agnostic" or "I believe all religions have truth" or to be otherwise uncommitted. Most of the time, these are a safe mask for ignorance of what these religions actually teach and certainly of the actual content of the Bible. If we don't recognize who Jesus is (and His identity is given us in Holy Scripture in stark clarity), if we are not continually in His Word, the world will have its way with us in all matters, not just our generation's particular traps (like sexuality). "Lord, keep us steadfast in Thy Word."

How Shall We Regard the Bible?

How shall Christians understand the Bible? The common narratives of Western culture are evaporating, especially knowledge of the Bible. Someone told me recently she was ordering a cake and wanted it decorated with a depiction of Noah's ark. The clerk had no idea what she was talking about.

Christians may still have a modicum of familiarity with the Bible, but today we ought be very clear about what the Bible is and teaches so we are not swept away by the cesspool of biblical ignorance (i.e., pop culture, pop religion, pop psychology).

Agnosticism is more popular than ever. It's the faddish pseudo-religion that asserts in absolute terms (ironically) that we can't make any absolute assertions about "God" or religion. Behind the masquerade of a religiously uncommitted "high ground"—claiming all religion is the same, etc.—lurks a chasm of ignorance about what the Bible and genuine Christianity teach.

The *best* place for us to get hold of what the Bible is and how to understand it is found in Jesus Himself. How does Jesus regard the Bible?

1. The Bible is about Jesus. Jesus cajoled His contemporaries who read the Bible but missed the point. "You search the Scriptures because you think that in them you have eternal life; and it is they that bear witness about me" (John 5:39). On the road to Emmaus, Jesus said, "'O foolish ones, and slow of heart to believe all that the prophets have spoken! Was it not necessary that the Christ should suffer these things and enter into his glory?' And beginning with Moses and all the prophets, he interpreted to them in all the Scriptures the things concerning himself" (Luke 24:25–27).

2. The Old Testament contains many prophecies about Christ: "'Everything written about me in the Law of Moses and the prophets and the Psalms must be fulfilled.' Then he opened their minds to understand the Scriptures, and said to them, 'Thus it is written, that the Christ should suffer and on the third day rise from the dead, and that repentance and forgiveness of sins should be proclaimed in his name to all nations'" (Luke 24:44–47).

3. The New Testament, especially the Gospels, is the accurate record of Jesus' life, death, resurrection and teaching, written by the power of the Holy Spirit. "These things I have spoken to you while I am still with you. But the Helper, the Holy Spirit, whom the Father will send in my name, he will teach you all things" (John 14:25–26).

4. Jesus regards what is written in the Old Testament as true. "Have you never read what David did?" (Mark 2:25). Jesus regards Adam, Eve, Jonah, Moses, etc., as actual people and events (Matthew 19:4ff.; 19:8).

5. Jesus believes that the writers of the Old Testament were inspired by the Holy Spirit. "David himself, in the Holy Spirit, declared, 'The Lord said to my Lord'" (Mark 12:36). His apostles had the same belief (Acts 4:25).

6. Jesus regards the Bible as the Word of God and authoritative. "For truly, I say to you, until heaven and earth pass away, not an iota, not a dot, will pass from the Law until all is accomplished" (Matthew 5:18).

7. Jesus believes that the commandments of the Old Testament are God's own. "You leave the commandment of God and hold to the tradition of men" (Mark 7:8).

8. Jesus regards the Scriptures as the Word of God that cannot be contravened, questioned or trumped by human authority or reason. "Scripture cannot be broken" (John 10:35).

9. Jesus understands the Bible according to Law and Gospel (i.e., God's commands and gifts of forgiveness, life and salvation), which point to Him as Savior. He piles on the Law when someone thinks the point of the Bible is works righteousness (Matthew 19:16ff.) but also tells His disciples that His reason for existence is not "to be served, but to serve and give his life as a ransom for many" (Matthew 20:28). Anyone who comes to Jesus empty-handed, begging for mercy, always goes away forgiven, healed, comforted (Mark 1:40ff.; 2:1ff.; 5:21ff.; 7:24ff.)! See Jesus' story of the Pharisee and the tax collector (Luke 18:9ff.) and then that of the rich young ruler (Luke 18:18ff.). Jesus told the first "to some

who trusted in themselves that they were righteous and treated others with contempt" (Luke 18:9). They'd missed the whole point of the Bible and Jesus!

A criticism of our teaching on the inerrancy and authority of the Bible is that we first must convince people of the Bible's authority and only then can the Gospel of forgiveness in Christ be shared and believed. Actually, it's the opposite. The message of damnable sin and complete forgiveness in the cross and resurrection of Jesus creates faith in Jesus. Such faith recognizes the voice of the Good Shepherd in the Scriptures: "My sheep hear my voice, and I know them, and they follow me" (John 10:27). As sheep precious to the Savior, we recognize the Bible to be what Jesus did: the very Word of God. "Long ago, at many times and in many ways, God spoke to our fathers by the prophets, but in these last days he has spoken to us by his Son" (Hebrews 1:1).

Entirely True, Accurately Given

Some 144 years ago, a seminary student in Bavaria wrote Dr. C. F. W. Walther with a troubled conscience. His Bavarian church was orthodox in its confession but was slipping badly in its practice. How long should one remain in a "corrupt" church? Dr. Walther responded, "Stay, be faithful, and make them throw you out." Young John Fackler ignored Walther's advice and, in fact, was soon studying at the St. Louis seminary and even living in Dr. Walther's home! I found this story so interesting I translated Walther's two letters to Fackler in *At Home in the House of My Fathers* (CPH, 2012; pp. 177ff.). But I had no idea where Fackler ended up serving in the Missouri Synod . . . until a few months back.

I had the pleasure of preaching for the 150th anniversary of St. John's, Corcoran, Minnesota. As I was preparing for this occasion, I learned that the founding pastor was—you guessed it—John Fackler! Imagine my surprise when, at the luncheon after the anniversary services, I met Myrtle Klemp, who, still spry at 99 years of age, told me, "I was baptized by Pastor Fackler! I knew him well as a child." Amazing!

Consider the dates of the events of the New Testament. Jesus is crucified in AD 33. St. Paul is converted in 36. His first missionary journey is in 46–47, the apostolic council (Acts 15) is in 48 or 49. Paul writes Galatians in 55; 1 Corinthians and 1 Timothy in 56; 2 Corinthians in 57; Romans and Titus in 58; Ephesians, Colossians and Philemon in 59; 2 Timothy in 60; and Philippians in 61. (These are the dates I've got scribbled in my Greek New Testament, taken from Bo Reicke's *Re-Examining Paul's Letters: The History of the Pauline Correspondence*, T&T Clark, 2008.) Dating the Gospels is more challenging, but suffice it to say that the generally accepted dates for authorship have been creeping closer and closer to the historical events of Jesus' ministry (i.e., 30–33). Reicke also noted that the only reason critics have asserted that the Gospels were written after AD 70 was that they contain Jesus' prophecies of the destruction of Jerusalem by Rome, which occurred in that year. The critics argue such prophecies had been placed in Jesus' mouth only after the fact. But just for the sake of argument, let's suppose that the Gospels were all written as late as AD 80.

My father-in-law is 90 years old (a decade younger than Myrtle). He was born in 1924. Transposing this century onto the first, Jesus would have begun His ministry in 1930, was crucified and risen in 1933. My father-in-law has vivid recollections of events from the late 1920s. He is also a WWII veteran and remembers helping to liberate Paris, returning home for a brief furlough after victory in Europe and preparing to ship out to the Pacific when the atom bomb was dropped. There are people all around us who are completely cognizant of events from 1930. Myrtle has vivid memories from before 1920! If I were to assert that the first resident pastor of St. John's Corcoran had been a thief or a drunk, a man who pastored that church in its early years, Myrtle would vigorously assert by personal experience that such an accusation is completely false.

Yet no one from within the Christian community took it upon themselves to write a refutation of the events recounted in the Gospels or Acts or even St. Paul's letters. Yes, there were some kooky Gnostic writings that were obviously spurious and written by individuals in heretical communities, most written well beyond the life-span of actual eyewitnesses. But no legitimate insider wrote something that said, "Hey, folks! I was with Jesus! I knew Paul! And these Gospels and letters of Paul are bogus! It didn't happen that way!" In fact, the *essential* criterion for acceptance of a New Testament document by the Church was whether or not it was known to be the product of an apostle or directly based upon apostolic witness (e.g., Luke/Acts).

This indicates that what I know to be so by faith—that is, the words of Jesus, the accounts of Jesus, His death and resurrection, and the words and works of the apostles—are entirely true and accurately given in the New Testament. Amazing. Joy indeed!

Why Read the Bible?

The Triune God speaks. The idols are dumb. When God speaks, things happen. "God said 'Let there be light,' and there was light" (Genesis 1:3). When the ancient prophets spoke the "word" of God about what was to come, it happened (1 Kings 13:32). The prophet Micah declared, "O you Bethlehem . . . from you shall come forth for me one who is to be ruler of Israel" (Micah 5:24), and it happened 700 years later! The Old Testament sometimes says that the mighty deeds of God are a "word" that is to happen (Isaiah 9:8). On the basis of John 1, the Early Church fathers believed that Jesus was the word "spoken" to create the world: "In the beginning was the Word and the Word was with God and the Word was God" (John 1:1). Jesus Himself is the "Word" *par excellence*: "In these last days he has spoken to us by his Son" (Hebrews 1:1). The word of Christ is given from the Father to the apostles: "For I [Jesus] have given them the words that you gave me and they have received them and have come to know the truth" (John 17:8).

What the Word of God says happens (see the horrid story of the end of Jezebel in 2 Kings 9:36–37). The Word of God doesn't merely predict happenings; it causes them to happen. "For He spoke and it came to be!" (Psalm 33:9). The Word always achieves its purpose. "By myself I have sworn . . . a word that shall not return; To me every knee shall bow, every tongue swear allegiance" (Isaiah 45:23). "Blessed be the Lord who has given rest to his people. . . . Not one word has failed of all his good promise which he spoke by Moses his servant" (1 Kings 8:56).

The Bible is actually the written Word of God. "No prophecy comes from one's own interpretation . . . but men spoke from God as they were carried along by the Holy Spirit" (2 Peter 1:21, concerning the Old Testament). Jesus promised His apostles, "But the Helper, the Holy Spirit, whom the Father will send in my name, he will teach you all things and bring to your remembrance all that I have said to you" (John 14:26, concerning the New Testament). And so they wrote it down. We believe, teach and confess that the written words of the prophets and apostles in the Bible are the inerrant, verbally inspired and effective Word of God Himself!

So what's the benefit of reading and knowing the Bible? So that the Word of God achieves its purpose in your life too. "The Word of the Lord does not return void" (Isaiah 55:11). The Word of God creates faith in Christ, and faith receives the Word (2 Corinthians 11:4). By the Word of the Gospel of Jesus Christ, the Spirit dwells in believers (1 Corinthians 3:16). The Word of God, preached but also read, is an action. In fact, it is the "power of God unto salvation" (Romans 1:16). The Word of God saves (Ephesians 1:13f.) and works rebirth, renewal (1 Peter 1:23) and hope (Colossians 1:5). The Word of God is the source for strength in life and its many challenges (Ephesians 6:5). It reminds us that we are nothing of ourselves—that we are all naked and exposed to the eyes of Him to whom we must give account (Hebrews 4:13)—and that God's Word is "sharper than any two-edged sword, piercing to the division of soul and spirit" (Hebrews 4:12f.). And that is exactly what we need now in these last wretched days. Luther often repeated that reason without faith is a problem because there are many challenging things in the Bible. "Faith speaks, I believe you Lord. . . . But what does God say? He says things that are impossible, false, stupid, inconsistent, absurd, abhorrent, heretical and diabolical if you consult your reason" (Weimar Edition, vol. 40/1, p. 361). But the Bible, which is a challenge to understand, carries its own solution to our dilemma and works faith.

Reading the Bible provides consolation and hope in these trying times. Christ said it would be so (Matthew 24–25). Reading the Bible helps us "give a reason for the hope that is within" (1 Peter 3:15). Reading the Bible directs us to seek preaching and the Sacraments (Hebrews 10:19ff.).

Many years ago I began to note that the elderly saints whose funerals I was conducting had confirmation verses that remarkably reflected their lives. It was uncanny. I used to think that those old pastors really had profound insight into the lives of these dear saints when they were young. I still think that's so, but there's more. I think that the Word of God in a confirmation verse actually has the power to shape a life and so often does. Such is the power of God's Word, especially the words of the very Gospel.

To Rome with Love

I appeal to Caesar" (Acts 25:11). Because of those words, St. Paul, a Roman citizen, found himself aboard a large Egyptian freighter carrying 276 people as it drifted without sail and tackle across the Mediterranean Sea for 14 days from Crete to the small island of Malta (Acts 27).

That's where I recently picked up the story, traveling with Rev. Dr. James Voelz of our wonderful Concordia Seminary and 25 travelers, tracing the journey St. Paul made to Rome around AD 57 and to the place where he would eventually face martyrdom. We experienced a number of moving moments as we traveled the route of Paul's journey, seeing the very places where he was held captive, proclaimed Christ, was under house arrest, was martyred and where his earthly remains, by all accounts, lay buried. But one repeated experience kept hammering something home to us.

Along the route, we visited ancient Greek temples. After three months on Malta, Paul and company set sail for Syracuse in Sicily. Today, a Catholic church stands just a hundred yards from the ancient port on top of a gently sloping hill. But that church was built as a pagan temple five centuries before Christ. The ancient form and pillars are unmistakable. It is more than likely that Paul and the Roman centurion Julius, to whom he was tethered by chain (Acts 27:1ff.), walked up that hill and viewed the temple and the city plaza.

We also visited the "Valley of the Temples" in Agrigento, where several of these massive structures still stand. They were built by thousands and thousands of slaves to worship the Greek and Roman gods and goddesses. In fact, half the population in the ancient Greco-Roman culture were slaves. Additionally, a huge number of priests and priestesses kept these large worship complexes in operation. One temple in Agrigento, now strewn across hundreds of yards of rubble, was some 270 feet long by 150 feet wide and 130 feet tall!

A visit to Herculaneum, which had been covered by the eruption of Mount Vesuvius in AD 79 and lay unknown under the volcanic mud and lava until the 18th century, was absolutely stunning. Then there was the "Forum of Appius," the "Three Taverns" (Acts 28:15) and finally . . . Rome. The Colosseum alone was testament to the ultimate power of the Roman Empire. For five centuries, "games" occurred, up to 170 days a year, where two teams of 24 gladiators fought until all but one remained. Do the math on the bloodshed. Horrid.

In the face of all this and much more—including sexual deviance and decadence, abortion and infanticide—stood one man with a message. "But whatever gain I had, I counted as loss for the sake of Christ. Indeed, I count everything as loss because of the surpassing worth of knowing Christ Jesus my Lord" (Philippians 3:7–8).

We stood in the church built over the home that Paul had rented with the help of the Philippians while he awaited trial in Rome. Luke ends Acts with these words: "He lived there two whole years at his own expense, and welcomed all who came to him, proclaiming the kingdom of God and teaching about the Lord Jesus Christ with all boldness and without hindrance" (Acts 28:30–31).

Paul wrote Philippians from that spot, and the foundations of that house are 30 feet below the church that stands there today. This little, and by his own account, unimpressive man proclaimed a message that rocked and conquered the most powerful kingdom on earth. And it happened one person at a time, sharing the message of Jesus one at a time—one Baptism at a time, one sermon at a time.

The verse that lit the Roman world and sparked the Lutheran Reformation is true still today: "The gospel . . . is the power of God for salvation" (Romans 1:16). Because it is a power hidden in weakness, because it is passed and believed one person at a time, because it is most often rejected, the life of sharing Christ is most often a very lonely path. But don't mistake for weakness this lowly and seemingly absurd message of Christ who died for our sins and was raised for our justification. With that message of Christ, the Church marches toward eternity and shall conquer hearts until the end of this world and all its kingdoms and their power, to the glory of God the Father.

Where Is Your God?

As classical Christians, we believe that the account of creation in Genesis records history. There is no middle ground here. You don't get very far with a real Adam in a mythical garden, or with a real fall into sin without a first human being. You can't stretch the accounts to cover billions or millions of years and so mesh the biblical account with Darwinism. The order of things created in Genesis does not even follow the order proposed by evolution. The problem of evil is unavoidable, and Darwin presumes death (a fallen state) as a presupposition to the development of human life (survival of the fittest). Genesis is either complete myth, or it is history recorded in the simple language of its time. . . .

Some years ago I found myself flat on my back in a dry, rock-strewn riverbed, hours from anywhere in central Australia. It was a crystal clear, pitch black, moonless night. I beheld the heavens in a spectacular, 3-D, high definition, life-sized, living, moving mural. It took my breath away. For the first time in my life, I beheld a whole galaxy. Horizon to horizon, a one-hundred-eighty-degree swath of a billion stars of the Milky Way, painted like glitter on a swath of black velvet, the blackness of deep space.

I was filled with doubt teetering on the edge of belief. "*Where is your God?*" (Psalm 42:10). In the face of infinity, how can I possibly believe that there is a God who is concerned about our tiny planet? How can I believe that there is a God who knows who I am and should even care about me or about any human being? Is there a God at all? Who and what am I? What is my life compared to the universe? I am a micro-speck, a piece of subatomic dust, circling a black hole—a minute piece of finitude, about to be devoured by infinity. "*When I look at your heavens, the work of your fingers, the moon and the stars, which you have set in place, what is man that you are mindful of him, and the son of man that you care for him?*" (Psalm 8:3–4).

But then I began to consider that all I beheld was marvelously ordered. "*Give thanks to him who made the great lights, for his steadfast love endures forever; the sun to rule over the day, for his steadfast love endures forever; the moon and stars to rule over the night, for his steadfast love endures forever*" (Psalm 136:8–9). I was staring God in the face, as it were. No, not God in the flesh, the revealed Son of God, but the same God in nature, nevertheless. *"Is not God high in the heavens?"* (Job 22:12). Yes, to be sure. But this is God who revealed Himself to Abram (who had the very same thoughts with which I struggle) and promised him, *"I will multiply your offspring as the stars of heaven. . . . And in your offspring all the nations of the earth shall be blessed"* (Genesis 26:4). God used the very thing that terrified Abraham to console him.

. . . And then I beheld, in my infinite insignificance, the Southern Cross, and my doubt was dashed upon the Bright and Morning Star (Revelation 22:16). *"He determines the number of the stars; he gives to all of them their names"* (Psalm 147:4). And the joy of knowing this God of the heavens in Christ chased back all doubt. *"And behold, the star that they had seen when it rose went before them until it came to rest over the place where the child was. When they saw the star, they rejoiced exceedingly with great joy"* (Matthew 2:9–10).

The secret to living a good news life in a bad news world is marveling with joy at the vast, ordered complexity of all creation and recognizing by faith the God (Father, Son, and Holy Spirit) who created it all for our blessed surprise, enjoyment, and faith.

—(Excerpted from *A Little Book on Joy* [CPH, 2011], pp. 99–107.)

The Church

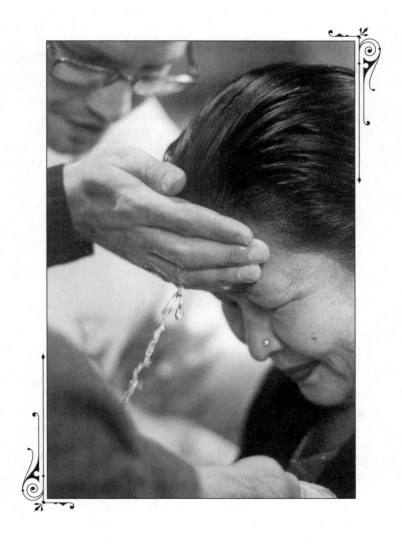

The Joy of Church

The Bible teems with joyous, paradoxical truths. God is three in one. God is man. God dies on a cross. The God who visits His vengeance upon trespassers has mercy only on sinners. We die to live. We live to die. The sinner is righteous. The weak are strong. Saints are sinners. Sinners are saints. Afflictions are blessings. The word of man is the Word of God. The poor are rich, and the rich are poor. The first are last, the last first. Law and Gospel. It is a hallmark of Lutheranism that it does not, as a matter of principle, try to resolve these paradoxes. Is it bread, or is it body? The texts simply state that it is both. If salvation is God's act alone, and faith is a result also of an eternal election to salvation (Ephesians 1), and God wants all to be saved, then why are not all saved? Must not God then have determined to condemn some from all eternity? No. The Bible says, "God wants all to be saved" (1 Timothy 2:4). Lutheranism lets the paradox stand. . . .

The maladies in the life of the twenty-first-century church, and in the Church in every age for that matter, are the result of missing "the narrow way" (Matthew 7:13–14). It is for me a paradox itself, that the "high" road of orthodoxy—right teaching and right praise—is freeing! For ortho-dox-y is both right doc-trine and right dox-ology (or praise). It also leaves plenty of space for us to rejoice in God-pleasing differences of gifts, emphases, practices and even personalities.

The Church is a paradox. She is the Bride of Christ, "spotless," "holy," "washed" (Ephesians 5:25–27), the "pillar and foundation of truth" (1 Timothy 3:15), the Body of Christ (1 Corinthians 12:1ff.). And yet she only appears in this world hidden under the guise of poor sinners, flawed leaders, tensions, divisions, and even false teaching. This is at once both disturbing and comforting. It is disturbing because we find ourselves in such "spotted" congregations, denominations and Christendom. It is comforting because—despite its outward appearance, despite the fact that there have been times in the history of the church when the pure teaching of the Gospel all but disappeared from the public confession of the Church and its practice—nevertheless, the "gates of hell shall not prevail against it" (Matthew 16:18). The Church endures because Christ endures, and He will never let His Gospel go unbelieved, until the end of time. That's worth rejoicing over, especially in the times in which we live. And there is also comfort in knowing that because the Church exists well beyond the genuine Lutheran Church, we will also find truth spoken by others. And when we do, we are free to heartily and gladly acknowledge it as such. . . .

The secret of living a good news life in a bad news world is knowing that despite our manifold weaknesses and sins, precisely of Christians and the Church, Christ remains wherever, so far and so long as, Christ and His Word are heard and to the extent that true Baptism and the Lord's Supper remain. That is the expansive joy of generous, faithful Lutheranism. Thus genuine Lutheranism is simply genuine Christianity. And Christianity, with all its manifold weaknesses and sins, is far broader than genuine Lutheranism. . . .

That's the joy of a generous, faithful Lutheranism—generous in recognizing the Church wherever the Gospel is, and faithful in recognizing its sacred duty to be faithful to the truth of God's Word. It may be a paradox, but it's a joyful paradox, nonetheless.

—(Excerpted from *A Little Book on Joy* [CPH, 2011], pp. 162–68.)

Where Is the Church?

"Although the true Church in the proper sense of the word is in its essence invisible, nevertheless its existence can be (definitely) recognizable, namely, by the marks of the pure preaching of God's Word and the administration of the Sacraments according to Christ's institution." (Thesis V from Walther's *Church and Office*)

My sainted teacher Rev. Dr. Kurt Marquart used to put it this way: "We cannot infallibly know the 'who' of the Church (because faith is unseen), but we can know the 'where.'" As Ignatius of Antioch put it: "Where there is Christ, there is the Church." The presence of the Church is not determined by a priesthood sanctioned by the papacy. The presence of the Church is not guaranteed by the morality of the church members. The presence of the Church is not guaranteed by an Office of the Ministry passed from minister to minister in succession. The presence of the Church is not guaranteed by a voters assembly. The presence of the Church is not guaranteed by the size of the congregation. The presence of the Church is not determined by the activity of individual members.

The presence of the Church is determined and guaranteed by Christ in His Word and Sacraments. Christ creates and sustains faith by these means. Where they are present and distributed, there is the Office of the Ministry and believers who receive these Means of Grace. This teaching is enormously comforting because in this life we are associated with Christians who are purely poor sinners, just like ourselves. They fail. We fail. Pastors fail. Some fail horribly. We are often loveless. Our righteous deeds are as filthy rags, as Isaiah says (64:6). Our congregations are often beset by controversy and conflict. Why? We are sinners, just like the apostles at the time of Jesus and just like the congregations in Galatia, Ephesus and Corinth. The beautiful and comforting teaching of the New Testament is this: the Church lives where Jesus is in His blessed Word and Sacraments. There faith is created. There is the Church.

Witness, Mercy, Life Together

Luther well knew what he was preaching on that St. Stephen's Day in 1523. He did not believe that the response of the apostolic church in Acts 6 to the problem of needy widows was merely a temporary glitch in the Church's life. Neither did C. F. W. Walther. Right from his earliest years in America, this text from Luther began to appear again and again in Walther's writings on the Church. Why? Our fathers and mothers in the faith knew Luther, and they knew the New Testament.

Dr. Walther asserts that the pastor is also to be concerned with the poor, the needy, and the weak *within* the congregation. And yet, he asserts that in times of need and disaster, the congregation is to be concerned with those *outside* the church. He refers to Galatians.

"When James and Cephas and John, who seemed to be pillars, perceived the grace that was given to me, they gave the right hand of fellowship [*koinonia;* LIFE TOGETHER] to Barnabas and me, that we should go to the Gentiles and they to the circumcised [WITNESS]. Only, they asked us to remember the poor, the very thing I was eager to do [MERCY]" (Galatians 2:9–10).

Here three things come together:

1. The apostles carefully resolved the doctrinal and practical challenges that always result from taking the Gospel to new peoples—for the sake of WITNESS to Jesus [Acts 15].

2. The apostles were deeply concerned that the Church be a locus of MERCY to those suffering physical need.

3. This witness and mercy were part and parcel of the Church's very life—yes, its LIFE TOGETHER.

This is the threefold key to the future of The Lutheran Church—Missouri Synod. Hear Luther:

> From this story (Acts 6) we learn in the first place how a Christian community should be constituted. In addition, we have a true pattern of spiritual government *[geistlichen Regiments]* that the apostles here provide. They care for souls, occupy themselves with preaching and prayer, and yet also see to it that the body is cared for; for they

47

suggest several men who are to distribute the goods, as you have heard. Thus the Christian rule is concerned for the people in both body and soul *[Leib und Seele]* so that no one suffers want . . . that all were richly fed and well cared for in both body and soul.

This is a very fine pattern and example, and it would be well for us to do likewise, if only the people were so minded. A city could be divided, as here, into four or five parts, and every part would receive a preacher *[Prediger]* and several deacons to supply the people with preaching, distribute the goods, visit the sick, and see to it that no one suffers want. But we do not have the persons for that. . . . A "bishop" means a steward *[Amtmann]* of God who is to distribute the divine and spiritual gifts, preach the Gospel, and supply the people with the Word of God. He must have ministers, and these are the deacons who serve the community in such a way that they have a list of all the poor people and care for them in all their needs with the money of the community, visit the sick, and in every way handle the supplies with great care.

("Sermon for St. Stephen's Day, Dec. 26, 1522"; WA 12:693ff.; quoted by Walther, *Church and Ministry,* Theses VIII, On the Ministry).

God grant it!

What Is It We Actually Share?

So, what is this "life together" in the Church? What does it mean that we in the Missouri Synod are "in this together"? And what finally holds us together anyway?

The answer to these questions would appear to be quite simple. We are like-minded religiously or at least enough to participate in a local congregation. We are comfortable together in this or that congregation. We are free to associate as we wish in this country and have freely decided to join our local LCMS church. Though we have many differences across the Synod, we share certain goals, and as free individuals and congregations, we freely decide to associate for worthy religious and charitable ends.

As much truth as there is in these answers, they certainly don't get at what the Bible says holds us together as Christian and truly Lutheran.

In the new threefold emphasis—WITNESS, MERCY, LIFE TOGETHER—this third aspect of life together is how we've rendered the New Testament word *koinonia*. The word means "participation," "having something in common," or "a sharing in something." Quite often in the writings of St. Paul, when he mentions this sharing, he also notes what is shared. Thus, "God is faithful, by whom you were called into the fellowship [*koinonia*] of his Son, Jesus Christ our Lord" (1 Corinthians 1:9). In other words, those "called into fellowship" share Jesus.

Now note who the actor is: "*God* is faithful." He's the One acting. He's doing the primary sharing too! What Jesus says to His apostles applies also to us: "You did not choose me, but I chose you" (John 15:16). "You were called (passive) into the fellowship of his Son." Because of God's action, God's doing, God's calling, we have been brought into a "fellowship," a "communion," a "sharing." As Paul notes, we share in "his Son, Jesus Christ our Lord."

This life in Christ—the vertical *koinonia* or sharing in Christ, created by *Him*—also creates a "life together" with others in Christ—the horizontal *koinonia*. Even with Christians with whom we do not share official church fellowship, we believe *koinonia* exists, though hidden. For we believe, with our Lutheran Confessions, that wherever Jesus is with His Word and Sacrament, there are believers (Preface to the Book of Concord), also far and wide outside the orthodox Lutheran Church, if only the Gospel is not totally eclipsed.

The great importance of *koinonia* as LIFE TOGETHER is marvelously displayed by St. Paul in 1 Corinthians 10–12, his great teaching chapters on the Lord's Supper and the Church. Paul writes, "The bread that we break, is it not a participation [*koinonia*] in the body of Christ?" In the Sacrament of the Lord's Supper, we share Christ's body and blood, so Paul continues: "Because there is one bread, we who are many are one body, for we all partake of the one bread" (1 Corinthians 10:17). From our sharing in Christ's body come very deep ethical ramifications. Because we are one body in Christ, "If one member suffers, all suffer together; if one member is honored, all rejoice together" (1 Corinthians 12:26; cf. Acts 2:42, 45; 4:32).

Luther wrote a splendid tract on this topic. In one of my favorite passages, he stated,

> This fellowship consists in this, that all the spiritual possession of Christ and his saints [i.e., believers] are shared with and become the common property of him who receives this sacrament. Again all sufferings and sins also become common property; and thus love engenders love in return and [mutual love] unites. (LW 35:51)

What do we share? What finally brings us together and holds us together? Jesus. And so we have a LIFE TOGETHER that includes a great array of important aspects and tasks (circuits, pastor and teacher conferences, Concordia Plan Services, seminaries and universities, reconciliation, CTCR and many others).

Our life together is a gift ("spiritual possession of Christ") and a gift to be tended ("love engenders love . . . and unites").

Concerning Visitation

A home going pastor makes a church going people." Those words of Dr. Robert Preus at the Fort Wayne seminary stuck with me. Before I began serving in my first parish, I had also stumbled across the section in Dr. Walther's *Pastoral Theology*, where he instructs pastors about the importance of and how to visit the homes of parishioners. Combined with good effort at preaching, there is simply nothing so significant in the pastor-people relationship and the well-being of the congregation as visitation.

Visitation is a much more profound reality for the Church than we realize. Just follow Jesus' movement through the Gospel of Mark. "Let's go!" He told His disciples (Mark 1:38). Jesus is the quintessential peripatetic. The "Great Commission" gives every pastor and the whole church its mission. It's no mistake that Matthew 28:19 is the first verse in the ordination rite. "Go, therefore!" After the Jerusalem Council sorted things out regarding the Gentile/circumcision question, Paul turned to Barnabas and said, "Let us return and *visit* the brothers in every city where we proclaimed the word of the Lord, and see how they are" (Acts 15:36). What is not evident in an English Bible is that the Greek word in the original for *visit* is the verb form of the word Paul uses for *overseer*—that is, *episcopus* or *bishop*. "Therefore an overseer [*episcopus*] must be above reproach, the husband of one wife, sober-minded, self-controlled, respectable, hospitable, able to teach" (1 Timothy 3:2).

Someone once quipped, "The problem with you Lutherans is not that you don't have any bishops. The problem is you have too many!" They were referring to the teaching of the New Testament and of our Lutheran Confessions that every local pastor is an overseer or bishop. What's his authority? Only the Word of God. And the chief word Paul uses to describe the pastor's office is the very word for *visit*! A pastor is a visitor. He admonishes, rebukes on occasion, consoles, encourages and comforts God's people—all with the Word of God—and he does it while wearing out his shoes, speaking the Gospel to those along the way who have not heard it.

Out of freedom, the Early Church followed the example of Jesus, Paul and the apostles in ordering the church. At the time of the Reformation, when most of the Catholic bishops did not become Lutheran, Luther and company began ordering the church for its benefit too. (See Luther's Works, vol. 40, p. 269.) From the beginning, the Lutherans called most of their bishops "superintendents," and the LCMS calls its leaders "presidents" (e.g., district president, Synod president).

The constitution and bylaws of the LCMS are heavily weighted toward visitation, a function of ecclesiastical oversight or supervision. That is a fundamental task of the Office of the Ministry. Our presidents are in the office, and they carry out the functions of the office as a ministry of service, which extends no further than the Word of God. In this, the district presidents are defined as an extension of the Synod president's office. The president of the Synod is to visit the districts, the universities and the seminaries and has general ecclesiastical supervision to see that the doctrine and practice of the Synod is adhered to and that convention decisions are carried out. "Doctrine and life!" (Luther). District presidents are to visit the congregations and pastors. To get this done, they are to use their vice-presidents and especially circuit counselors. We should return to calling these men "circuit visitors." One sees a "counselor" when there is a problem, but visitation is to be a regular form of pastoral encouragement toward fidelity and mission, accountability, admonition, comfort and care. Just check out Paul's letters to figure out what it's all about. He went. He sent letters. He sent co-workers. As he visited established churches, he constantly preached and planted new ones.

Absent visitation, we paralyze the "legs of the Gospel" as it were—whether it be parish pastor, circuit counselor, district president or Synod president. Visit!

Baptized for This Moment

Someone once said, "Courage is faith that has said its prayers." I prefer to say, "Courage is fear that has been baptized!" The theme for this summer's LCMS convention [2013] is "Baptized for This Moment." The theme verse is from the great missionary book of the New Testament, the Acts of the Apostles. "Repent and be baptized every one of you in the name of Jesus Christ for the forgiveness of your sins, and you will receive the gift of the Holy Spirit. For the promise is for you and for your children and for all who are far off, everyone whom the Lord our God calls to himself" (Acts 2:38b–39).

If ever the Church has needed courage, it is now. But as an armchair historian, I'm familiar enough with what Christians have written and experienced through the centuries. There is a common theme from Paul's epistles to Luther to C. F. W. Walther: "Things can hardly get worse! We are in the very last days, and Jesus will return soon!" "Amen! Come, Lord Jesus!" (Revelation 22:20). So as bad as things may look to us now, "No temptation has overtaken you that is not common to man" (1 Corinthians 10:13). Indeed, the Lord has blessed and preserved the Church through all the centuries, and Jesus promised that "the gates of hell shall not prevail against it!" (Matthew 16:18).

In all of history, this is the moment the Lord has given us. Like Luther standing in front of the powers of the Western world when he gave his "Here I stand" speech, we stand in the face of "principalities and powers" of darkness (Ephesians 6:12). The devil knows his time is short, and his attacks are intense, especially upon the Missouri Synod (Revelation 20:7f.; Matthew 24:24). The devil and our sinful flesh would lull us into apathy over the Gospel and do anything to decrease our passion and zeal for proclamation of the Gospel to those who need Christ, tempting us to believe that, having it all correct, we can smugly sit back and keep our light under a bushel, hoping that a few parched souls might stumble upon us (Matthew 5:15; 22:2f.). Or we might be tempted to jettison portions of God's Word and our confession for the sake of mission—a kind of mission reductionism (Matthew 28:20; Acts 20:27). If the devil can set confession against mission or mission against confession, he's got us! The two belong together (1 John 4:14–15).

The convention theme verse has something to say to us all.

"Repent!" I love to confess the sins of someone else! "I thank thee that I'm not like other men!" (Luke 18:11). It's time for me to confess *my* sins of apathy, coldness toward the Gospel, lack of love for my neighbor who needs Christ, apathy for the fellowship of which the Lord has made me a part and so on.

"Be baptized every one of you in the name of Jesus!" "I am baptized" was Luther's greatest comfort. Despite my sins and manifest and manifold failings, God has grabbed me by the neck, sinner that I am, and made me His own (Titus 3:5).

"For the forgiveness of your sins." I'm forgiven! I forgive! (Read *all* of Matthew 18.)

"And you will receive the gift of the Holy Spirit." I have the Spirit of Christ. I recognize the Word of my Savior in Holy Scripture (John 10:27). I have comfort in affliction (Matthew 11:28). I have courage in duress (John 14:27)! I can speak the Word of God to my neighbor (1 Peter 2:9).

"The promise is for you and your children, for all who are far off, and everyone whom the Lord will call." I have a promise, God's own promise in Christ! His blood sealed it. The promise is for me and my family and for *all* whom the Lord will call. And just how does the Lord do His calling? Through His Word preached from pulpits and shared by everyone in his or her vocation, whether missionary or humblest father, mother, son, daughter or friend (Romans 10:8).

Have courage! We are *baptized* for this moment. And courage is fear that has been baptized.

Unifying Solutions

A nd let the peace of Christ rule in your hearts, to which indeed you were called in one body. And be thankful" (Colossians 3:15). Remarkable! Paul says Christians are called to "let the peace of Christ rule in your hearts." And even more, we are called "in one body," collectively for the peace of Christ to rule us all together. Now, let's be clear: "I cannot by my own reason or strength believe in Jesus Christ, my Lord, or come to Him; but the Holy Spirit has called me by the Gospel. . . . In the same way He calls, gathers, enlightens, and sanctifies the whole Christian Church on earth" (Luther's Small Catechism, explanation of the Third Article).

The actor is God. He's called and given us faith in Christ. Paul in Colossians is saying, "God has made you who you are. Now be who you are!"

Not too long ago, I dared to assert that I thought it possible for the Synod to be 85 percent united on even the difficult issues which often divide us. Can this happen? Coming into this summer's LCMS convention [2013], we worked very hard to bring unifying resolutions. When resolutions dealt with challenging issues where different parties were very much at odds, we worked even harder to bring people together and to come to reasonable and faithful compromise. Rather remarkable things happened, often behind the scenes. We were blessed with a very peaceful and productive convention.

It's my conviction that the less time, energy and money we spend on internal disagreement, the more we can focus on our domestic and international opportunities, which are legion! But we can't simply shout "Mission!" as a mere distraction for the work of living our unity. We need to be confronted with God's inerrant Word, and that Word must have its way with us. I'm convinced that the historic and time-honored biblical positions of the LCMS are unifying. They are Gospel-centered and tested.

The convention was really remarkable in that the vast majority of resolutions passed with overwhelming majorities of 90 percent or more. Many passed unanimously! Very significant and potentially controversial resolutions on issues like visitation and close(d) Communion passed in the high 70s. We are blessed, truly blessed.

As this next triennium unfolds, our task will be to work toward reasonable consensus on issues that have continued to trouble and divide, such as SMP and the licensed deacon programs. We must work toward unifying solutions that are faithful to the Scriptures and the Lutheran Confessions, solutions that are wise and that find the path of good order serving the Gospel, recognizing legitimate Christian freedom. By God's grace, we can do it.

Standing in front of 1,500 LCMS delegates was a humbling experience. More than once I was reduced to embarrassment over my lack of parliamentary skill. The vice-presidents felt the same way, I'm sure. But more than anything else, I was profoundly thankful. The work of the floor committees was just remarkable. Those who felt negatively affected by this or that resolution carried themselves in Christian fashion and made their views known and heard. The "Baptized for This Moment" theme galvanized the body as preacher after preacher and Bible study leader after Bible study leader drove home the biblical case for Baptism's extraordinary ramifications for our real lives. Delegates were patient with me and each other. They were gracious. They were in constant good humor. They demonstrated a deep love for the Gospel of free forgiveness in Jesus and for The Lutheran Church—Missouri Synod. And when it all ended, the room was filled with deep joy and thanksgiving.

The Missouri Synod has her warts, to be sure. But she's the best thing going. I will continue to do my level best to keep you informed about what's going on (mission, numbers, money, giving, program). As we continue into the future Christ has in store for us, I pledge you my prayers for all our pastors, church workers and congregations. And I plead for yours, that Paul's entreaty be true of all of us: "And let the peace of Christ rule in your hearts, to which indeed you were called in one body. And be thankful."

Beloved Synod, Take Courage!

There is unfolding before us a moment of opportunity for The Lutheran Church—Missouri Synod like nothing ever before in our history. We have a worldwide vocation, a world that is calling us to account, to stand and be counted for Christ. Despite all our weaknesses, we have unbelievable worldwide capacity for the advancement of the Gospel and the Lutheran Confessions. It's a moment for courage. Shall we dare, by faith in Christ, to seize the moment?

We are beset by deep challenges on every front. The financial struggles of our nation pinch our schools and churches, as well as our district and national work. The world presses us hard as much of Western Christianity settles gradually into a more biblical, albeit minority, status (Matthew 7:13–14). Our strength seems to pale in the face of a virulent Islam, an aggressive and ubiquitous Mormonism or the barrage of secular garbage delivered by the media 24/7 right into our homes. Christian courage is in short supply. Where shall we find the fortitude to go on the offensive in these last and wretched days?

Circa 800 BC, Elisha the prophet unveiled to a cowering army of the Lord its hidden but real strength.

> When the servant of the man of God rose early in the morning and went out, behold, an army with horses and chariots was all around the city. And the servant said, "Alas, my master! What shall we do?" He said, "Do not be afraid, for those who are with us are more than those who are with them." Then Elisha prayed and said, "O Lord, please open his eyes that he may see." So the Lord opened the eyes of the young man, and he saw, and behold, the mountain was full of horses and chariots of fire all around Elisha. (2 Kings 6:15–17)

And so it is with us. Lord, open our eyes! As with the cross itself, the countenance of the Church in this world is always weakness. The Church is always hidden under affliction, beset with challenges, struggling with divisions. It is always apparently outnumbered in battle. It has never been otherwise. This truth is portrayed on almost every page of the Bible. And yet, "On this rock [Peter's confession of Christ] I will build my Church, and the gates of hell shall not prevail against it" (Matthew 16:18).

Luther taught that because of our certainty of forgiveness and God's reckoning us righteous on account of Jesus, we are free to live this Christian life with a "joyful daring," a joyful courage! Luther said there are three things that produce courage in the Christian:

1. *Repentance.* Confessing our sins daily, we have a clear conscience. We're not paralyzed by guilt or anger or regret. We are forgiven and freed to act (1 Peter 3:21; Acts 23:1).

2. *We have a clear Word of God.* The Bible is a clear book. It is God's own Word, and we have in the Sacred Scriptures everything we need for faith and life. There is no need to wallow in indecision. We can act with divinely wrought confidence (Daniel 10:19; Romans 15:4)!

3. *Vocation.* The Lord calls us into His Church to live our lives where He has placed us individually (Romans 1:6; 1 Corinthians 7:20). Our service to Jesus does not entail running away from the people in our family, community or church. We are called to evangelize and love precisely *them!*

And the Missouri Synod, therefore, has a collective vocation. Our ecumenical task is to hold forth worldwide for orthodox, biblical Christianity—for the singular authority of Holy Scripture; for the singular truth that salvation is completely by grace (a gift!) on account of Christ's meritorious life, death and resurrection for us; for the singular truth that this gift is grabbed hold of solely by faith, which is itself worked completely by God through His Word.

Finally, we have a vocation to strengthen worldwide Lutheranism in its witness to Christ for the salvation of souls. This is a moment like never before. The sexuality decisions of the ELCA and European Lutherans, the shrinking world linked by travel and instant communication—all are sending worldwide Lutheranism to our door. And much of Lutheranism wants precisely what the LCMS has: the solid confession of Christ in the midst of a world of sweeping uncertainty.

Take courage! Let's go on the offensive! "Do not be afraid, for those who are with us are more than those who are with them."

Courage Is Fear That Has Been Baptized

There are plenty of reasons for us to fear the future. The favored status of the Church in our culture is ebbing away from us. In some places in our country, open hostility to Christianity has long held sway, and many of our members experience this secular derision on a daily basis. The united front on basic ethical issues once enjoyed by the entire Lutheran Church in this country is now gone. The devilish attack on marriage from all angles is bearing its hellish fruit as a result of the elimination of moral standards, unleashing a flood of sexual confusion, pornography, destructive live-in relationships, divorce, abuse and more. The dear folks of the Missouri Synod are not immune to any of these things, as we well know. The flood of immigration has brought strange religions en masse to every corner of this country. Humanly speaking, there is every reason for fear.

The Lutheran Church—Missouri Synod is sorely pressed. Thirty years ago, when I graduated from high school, the pool of youth in our church body numbered some 210,000. Today, the number is 90,000. This is because our birthrate has simply mirrored that of the broader European-descent population, and mission gains have not kept up with the decline in growth by birth. As a church body, we continue to be pressed hard by division over mission methods, limits of freedom in worship, Communion practice and more—all, in part, symptoms of the soup of religious pluralism and relativism in which we swim daily. The single most challenging aspect of being Synod president is having the facts about and facing these stark challenges and dozens more every day. Still, with the psalmist I pray, "Though an army encamp against me, my heart shall not fear; though war arise against me, yet I will be confident" (Psalm 27:3). But why?

It's been said that "Courage is fear that has said its prayers." I prefer "Courage is fear that has been baptized." It's no good ignoring the reality of the stiff challenges we face. But here we remember what Jesus said, "I have said these things to you, that in Me you may have peace. In the world you will have tribulation. But take heart; I have overcome the world" (John 16:33).

Martin Luther maintained a marvelous sense of humor in the midst of horridly tumultuous times. Why? As one scholar put it, he knew that since the ultimate is sure, the penultimate is no longer deadly serious. Jesus *has* overcome the world, and He's tied that victory to us. Fear + Baptism = Courage. Indeed, as next year's [2013] convention theme puts it, we are "Baptized for This Moment." We have a serious vocation. We've been placed on this earth—in this orthodox Lutheran church body at this very time of trial—to carry out our lives fully for the sake of a high, eternal purpose. We are here because of, for the sake of, the Gospel of Jesus Christ—the message of free forgiveness in Jesus' blood. And we know the end game. Jesus wins. In fact, He's already won.

It is in light of this victory that this issue of *The Lutheran Witness* seeks to set the facts on the "State of the Synod" right under your nose. There are challenges aplenty, but there are many, many blessings and things over which to rejoice. You'll see them on every page.

In light of all this:

- It's time to get our financial houses in order for the sake of the Gospel, starting with the national church. And we've taken huge steps in that direction.

- It's time for a renewal of preaching by which brother pastors are encouraged and built up, equipped to speak a clear word of Law and Gospel to every situation and every person inside and outside the Church.

- It's time for a renewal of visitation, the bedrock of pastoral practice and the bedrock of oversight in the Lutheran Church. That means home visitation by pastors; visitation of neighborhoods, immigrants, family, friends and the needy by all of us; visitation of parishes by circuit visitors and district presidents; and visitation of district and Synod entities by the Synod president—so we can all up our game for the sake of the Gospel.

- It's time to take a deep breath in the face of divisive issues and revisit the Scriptures, the Lutheran Confessions and the basic biblical principles we all have sworn to uphold.

- It's time to come together as a church body. We are in this together. The baptismal language in Paul is all plural for a reason! I saw a bumper sticker yesterday: "Want to get rich quick? Count your blessings!" It's time to count our blessings as a church. And boy, do we have them (seminaries, missions, mercy, schools, Foundation, LCEF, LWML, youth)!

- It's time to "set our face toward Jerusalem" with the very determination of Christ, realizing that every situation which we might view as negative (population shifts, immigration, pluralism, family breakdown) is actually a potential positive. When Rome fell to the barbarians, people thought that church and culture were at an end. Yet my ancestors (and most of yours) were the very "barbarians" who were seeking refuge across Roman borders, and in so doing, encountered the Gospel. "God meant it for *good*!"

In short, it's time for courage.

We Need Christmas

Someone asked me the other day what I hoped to see by the end of my tenure as Synod president. I thought for a moment and responded. It is my deepest desire that the Synod be strengthened theologically (a deepened commitment to Holy Scripture and our Lutheran Confessions); that the Synod be at peace, living in love toward one another and concentrating on her mission to reach the lost; that the Synod be financially transparent and vastly strengthened; and that the Synod's global mission and partner footprint be greatly expanded for the sake of the pure Gospel of Christ.

These rather simple goals can be accomplished by no one person, nor 8,000 clergy, nor all our church workers and not even by 2.3 million church members. The extent to which we edge forward in each of them is and shall be the result of divine gifts and blessings. How the pressures, challenges and difficulties we face in this world fill me with foreboding about the future! How our secularized culture presses hard on the Church and even into the Church! When problems in the LCMS reach my desk, they are often intractable.

On Christmas Day, 1534, Dr. Luther preached a brief sermon in his home (the large old monastery) to gathered family, friends and guests. He concluded it with just what you and I need to hear today, all these years later. He preached on the birth of Christ (Matthew 1; Luke 2).

> We should learn our lesson well and earnestly
> ponder the great honor that has been bestowed on
> us by Christ's becoming a human being. For it is
> such a great honor, that even if one were an angel,
> you would do well to wish that you were a human
> being, so that you could boast: My own flesh and
> blood is greater than all the angels, and blessed
> is every creature that is a human being. God grant
> that we understand this, take it to heart and thank
> God for this great gift. In addition, we should dili-
> gently study the example of Christ, what he mani-
> fested with his first advent to this earth in that he
> suffered for our sake, so that we too do our best
> to learn from him how to suffer. The Lord of all

lords becomes a Servant of all servants. We should follow that example and learn from our dear kinsman and brother to gladly help and serve other people, even when it becomes a burden for us and causes us to suffer a little bit in rendering that service. These two things we should note well: the account itself and the example it sets. To that end may God help us by the Holy Spirit through our dear Lord Jesus Christ. Amen. (*Sermons of Martin Luther: The House Postils* [Grand Rapids: Baker, 1996], vol. 1, p. 137)

Christmas teaches that Christ was born for us and suffered for our sake. And we learn from Him how to suffer and live a life of service to our neighbors wherever God has placed us. Knowing this, I sing a joyful "O Come, O Come, Emmanuel"; pause to receive Christ's gifts for forgiveness at church; and leave with a clear conscience, strengthened to suffer and serve. And I leave the results of that service to God and His good pleasure.

Persecution: Good for the Church

Not long after Johann Esch and Heinrich Voes were burned at the stake in Brussels on July 1, 1523, the news came to Luther. It disturbed him greatly that these two young men, monks of his Augustinian order who had confessed the Gospel of free forgiveness, were the first to die. Luther, after all, was responsible for the uproar. Why had the Lord not taken him?

The incident moved Luther and loosed his pen, and he wrote his first hymn: "A New Song Shall Here Be Begun." It's never made it into our hymnals because it is a type of ballad that the town minstrels would use, long before there were such things as newspapers, to take the latest news from town to town in sung form.

The 20th century was the bloodiest in Christian history with the death of tens of millions at the hands of Communist regimes. Now, we are continuously shocked by Islamic radicals persecuting and killing Christians daily in the Middle East and Africa. Meanwhile, our consciences vacillate as we sense the cultural shift in the US that has produced an increasing avalanche of harassment and is likely to get much worse.

I was in Ethiopia a few months back. In 1979, the leader of the Ethiopian Evangelical Church Mekane Yesus (now approaching seven million Lutherans) was murdered by the Communist government. I chatted at lunch with the current president and general secretary of the church. The topic of persecution came up. Mind you, each of these men had themselves been repeatedly jailed in the Communist period for their confession of Christ. I cannot begin to imagine the horror of an Ethiopian prison. President Wakseyoum Idosa leaned toward me across the table, raised his index finger, and said with all gravity, "Persecution is always good for the Church. Always."

Since Luther's hymn of martyrs is so unknown, I offer it to you as a hymnic/devotional prelude as you consume this issue of the *Witness*. I bid you pray for the modern martyrs soon to face death in Nigeria and elsewhere today. I bid you consider that your own "light momentary affliction is preparing for us an eternal weight of glory beyond all comparison" (2 Corinthians 4:17). From Calvary itself, we know that God works the very greatest things through suffering and martyrdom—a "new song," indeed.

A New Song Shall Here Be Begun

1. A new song now shall be begun,
Lord, help us raise the banner
Of praise for all that God has done,
For which we give Him honor.
At Brussels in the Netherlands
God proved Himself most truthful
And poured His gifts from open hands
On two lads, martyrs youthful
Through whom He showed His power.

7. A paper given them to sign—
And carefully they read it—
Spelled out their faith in ev'ry line
As they confessed and said it.
Their greatest fault was to be wise
And say, "We trust God solely,
For human wisdom is all lies,
We should distrust it wholly."
This brought them to the burning.

12. Let men heap falsehoods all around,
Their sure defeat is spawning.
We thank our God the Word is found,
We stand in its bright dawning.
Our summer now is at the door,
The winter's frost has ended,
Soft bud the flowers more and more,
By our dear Gard'ner tended
Until He reaps His harvest.

—Tr. F. Samuel Janzow, 1913–2001, published by Concordia Publishing House, 1982. Order *Martin Luther: Hymns, Ballads, Chants, Truth* from Concordia Publishing House to read all 12 stanzas.

Does the Lutheran Reformation Have a Future?

Five hundred years ago this month [October 2015], 32-year-old Martin Luther lived as a monk in Wittenberg. He earned his doctorate and soon began lecturing on the Psalms and Romans and would eventually preach well over 2,000 sermons in the City Church before he died in 1546. What began with Luther studying and lecturing on Scripture eventually led to an explosion that rocked the Christian world and continues to do so. That explosion can be summarized by the three "solas" —that salvation is free by grace alone, apprehended by faith alone and believed from Scripture alone.

As we approach the 500th anniversary of the Reformation in 2017, you will increasingly see reports of what Luther and his message meant and means today. So what is the Reformation? Hermann Sasse described it as an episode in the history of the *Church*. It is foremost about the *Church* of Jesus Christ. "All [other] attempts to explain the Reformation are abortive . . . because they do not approach the Reformation from that point of view from which alone it can be understood—from the point of view of the reality of the church" (Sasse, *Here We Stand* [Harper, 1938], p. 50).

What's going on with the Church today? Liberal Protestantism is collapsing worldwide. Rome is busy nuancing its image with a very active pope, yet also churning out new indulgences as though there had never been a Reformation. The Lutheran World Federation (LWF) and liberal American and European Lutherans are busy reinterpreting the Reformation as though it were the impetus for the full and final acceptance of homosexuality, bisexuality, transgenderism, etc., in the Church. The LWF has a full-scale "hermeneutics" project to convince Lutherans in the Global South that the Bible doesn't really mean what it means or that it may mean something different in the South than in the North, and we all should just let it mean what it means to each of us and be happy about it.

Fortunately, many in the South are not buying it. As an episode in church history, this anniversary of the Reformation may be part of the greatest revival of the Church, and certainly the Lutheran Church, since the Reformation itself. We in the LCMS have so many requests for dialogue, partnership and church fellowship that we can't keep up. These are from huge churches like the Mekane Yesus of Ethiopia and smaller but substantial churches in Ukraine and Norway and elsewhere. What do these churches want? How do they interpret the Reformation? *Sola gratia. Sola fide. Sola scriptura!* They want the Gospel. They want clear Lutheran teaching, based squarely on the clear Scriptures.

The real story of the Reformation is about the march of the Church of Jesus Christ in the face of impossible odds—thirsting for Christ and His Means of Grace, trusting in the Bible as God's inerrant Word, struggling in the North but growing tremendously in the South. The Lord's Church is one Church, facing Islam and secularism—strong in the weakness of Christ, confident of eternal life.

The Reformation was a movement of repentance. The first thesis of the Ninety-Five Theses reads: "When our Lord and Master Jesus Christ said 'repent,' he willed that the entire life of the Christian be one of repentance." There is much to repent of in our lives: greed, impure thoughts, gossip, faithlessness. There is much to repent of as a Church: shoddy Communion practice; lack of responsible visitation; gossip; second-rate preaching; inadequate teaching of the faith (e.g., one-day instruction classes to join the church); poor relationships among church staff; lack of care for pastors and church workers; lack of Bible class attendance; poor Bible class preparation; disdain for our magnificent Lutheran Confessions; lack of outreach and visitation of members and prospective members; lack of zeal for outreach and sharing the marvelous Gospel of Christ with our unchurched and dechurched neighbors. "Repent!" (Matthew 3:1ff.; 4:17ff.).

Does this make you angry? Have you nothing to repent of? When I write these things, I think of my own horrid guilt, not yours. Perhaps a dose of Reformation theology would do us both good. Here's what Luther wrote to his friend Spenlein in April 1516: "Beware of aspiring to such purity that you will not wish to be looked upon as a sinner, or to be one. For Christ dwells only in sinners" (Tappert, *Letters of Spiritual Counsel* [Philadelphia, Westminster], p. 110).

If "Christ dwells only in sinners," you'd better be one. The future of the Church does not depend upon us sinners. The Reformation has a future. Even more, the Church has a future because, as Sasse noted, Jesus Christ has a future.

Back to Walther!

It is always a sign of a deep spiritual sickness when a church forgets its fathers" (Hermann Sasse). Why? Because the life of the Church on this earth is always a forward trajectory—informed by, pushed forward by, anchored by the past. Life, and especially the Christian's life of repentance and faith, is a constant review of events occurred—sin committed, lived, suffered and confessed for forgiveness. What remains of yesterday's life is not to be a burden. Forgiveness is all about freedom, relieving the burden for the sake of today's confident trek into the future, all under God's grace. The eye on the past is a lesson learned for tomorrow. To know where we are going, we'd better have some idea whence we've come.

The greatest eras in the Church, the great times of advancement, always begin with the cry "Back to the Scriptures!" "Back to the fathers!" "Back to Luther!" Note how often God's faithfulness to our "fathers" is mentioned in the Psalms as a comfort to give courage in the present. "In you our fathers trusted. They trusted and you delivered them" (Psalm 22:4). Hilkiah found the lost Book of the Law (Deuteronomy?), and good King Josiah commenced a time of repentance and restoration (2 Kings 22).

Jesus anchored His ministry in the ancient prophets: "Today this scripture [Isaiah] is fulfilled in your hearing" (Luke 4:21). The ancient words of the Fathers were on the lips of Jesus at all the decisive moments of His life sacrificed for us: "My God, my God! Why . . ." (Psalm 22:1; Matthew 27:46). John the Baptizer was the "voice crying in the wilderness" spoken of by Isaiah (Matthew 3:3; Isaiah 40:3). Luther's message was "Back to the Scriptures!" and an explosion of fidelity to and understanding of the pure Gospel commenced. The greatest forward advancement of the Gospel has always begun with the cry "Back to the Scriptures! Back to the fathers!"

C. F. W. Walther was a reformer in this tradition. *Gottes Wort und Luthers Lehr, vergehet nun und nimmermehr!* ("God's Word and Luther's doctrine shall not pass away now or forever!") That's the statement Walther put on the masthead of his newspaper, *Der Lutheraner* ("The Lutheran") already in 1844.

The ravages of the Enlightenment had reached a low point in the German church just as Walther left Germany with a strange and even fanatic expedition bound for failure. But out of the wreckage, Walther was thrown upon Scripture, the Lutheran Confessions and the writings of Luther. "Back to Luther!" And from the ruins of failure came new life, new beginnings. "When God makes alive He does it by killing" (Luther's Works, vol. 33, p. 62). The result was this Missouri Synod.

By God's grace, and a lot of help from other faithful men and women, Walther founded a church in 1847 squarely and firmly upon the sacred and inerrant Scriptures and the Lutheran Confessions with a conviction that Luther got the Gospel right. Sasse once pointed out that largely because of the tenacity of Walther and the Missouri Synod, all of American Lutheranism had formally accepted the entire Book of Concord by the 400th anniversary of the Reformation in 1917.

We've wavered now and then. But the foundation was built so well that today—despite all our many weaknesses and faults—the LCMS remains committed to the same confession of faith because it's true.

As we push forward under the grace of God, let's recheck our foundation this 200th anniversary of C. F. W. Walther's birth [2011]. If we fail to understand Walther and our roots, what we build today may well squander what was given us by our fathers. And what we build today may look ever so marvelous and 21st-century-sleek, but soon may be frayed and flapping in the wind with no enduring basis.

"Forward" I say! And that means back to Walther! And Walther will tell us, "Back to Scripture! Back to the Lutheran Confessions! Back to Luther!"

Congregational Life

Pastor and Congregation 101

The basics of a pastor maintaining a healthy relationship with his congregation are not complex:

1. Preach a decent sermon (2 Timothy 4:1–5).

2. Love and visit your people (1 Peter 5:2–4), and pray for them!

3. Be visible in your community (1 Timothy 3:7).

When things aren't going well, sermons can become temptations to deliver subtle or even veiled messages to antagonists, visitation (even of shut-ins) can slow or cease and pastors may begin to absent themselves from the community (church and beyond), which they may perceive as unsupportive or even threatening.

Likewise, being a healthy congregation with respect for the pastor is simple too:

1. Love and care for your pastor (especially pray for him!).

2. Openly address concerns and be clear about expectations, starting with the list of passages in the ordination/installation rite. (See *LSB Agenda*, pp. 160–81.)

3. Confront and call to repentance members of the congregation who are disruptive and undermine the ministry of the congregation, especially through gossip and lack of charity.

All this is quite simple, but it all becomes very complex in real life, as we've all seen.

It does happen that a pastor may be called to a congregation that has a history of poor practice based on a weak or even wrong doctrinal understanding. Let's be honest. Our seminary graduates are taught the position of the Synod (and we believe the Scriptures and Confessions) that non-LCMS members should not ordinarily be communed. But a graduate may well be called to a congregation that has been communing non-Lutheran folks every week at the rail for decades! It's a touchy subject. If a young pastor doesn't have the best people skills, is a bit insecure and elects to try to change things too soon, it's likely to be a disaster. Both seminaries have been working very, very hard to prepare students for these and many other challenges. Part of that preparation is helping graduates to understand themselves and how they are likely to react to challenging and potentially conflicted situations. Not only new pastors, but experienced pastors get into problems in congregations when they push forward change too quickly. As a Synod, walking together, it's particularly important as a congregation is preparing to call a pastor that the circuit counselor, vacancy pastor or even district president let the congregation know (very charitably, to be sure) that its practice in this or that area needs to improve before it calls a new pastor.

Satan absolutely loves it when he can twist and distort the relationship between pastor and people. If he can set people a-gossiping, if he can get them to lambaste their pastor, especially to people *outside* the church, he's giddy with delight. He knows that no disgruntled congregant is going to be doing any inviting to church, much less evangelism. Griping is much more pleasing to the flesh. Satan knows that if he can bring enough angst to a pastor's life, wife and family, he might even pick off the shepherd and cause the sheep to scatter for good! If the old devil can cause an impatient pastor, who needs to grow in his knowledge and application of the Scriptures, to bring the hammer down and lead by coercion and not conviction, it's a short trip to congregational chaos. If Satan can get a pastor to wrap himself in the church's confession while being absolutely unwilling to confess that he's not Jesus and could have acted more patiently, could have been a much better teacher, could be much more diligent in visitation, could improve his preaching skills—then the trap's been sprung, and the devil is laughing all the way to hell.

Pastors and people, check out the ordination and installation rites in the *LSB Agenda* (pp. 160–81). Pastor, the first word of the first verse spoken over you is "Go" (Matthew 28:19). That one word is enough to cause me lamentation in my own ministry. How I've failed! People, on the basis of Hebrews 13:17, you promised that you would support your pastor "by your gifts and pray for him always that in his labors he may retain a cheerful spirit and that his ministry among you may be abundantly blessed." How have you failed? Repent. Believe the Gospel. Resolve to do better by the grace of God.

Pastors, Love Your People!

I t was a bright, crisp morning at the Graham and Gwen Koch sheep operation in Australia, just on the South Australia/ Victoria border. This wonderful, humble Lutheran couple managed several thousand sheep on several thousand acres. Graham piled us into his "ute," short for "utility vehicle" (we call it a "flatbed pickup" in Iowa). As we neared the flock, a thousand skittish animals began bawling and fleeing, a sea of nervous wool. But then the scene changed in an instant. Graham began calmly, even quietly, repeating, "Hey Bob. Hey Bob." Suddenly the flock turned toward us at once, and within a minute or two, we were in a sea of calm but bleating sheep. They were so tightly packed around the truck that I might have walked across them. The sheep knew his voice (John 10:3). It was a magic moment of profound joy and New Testament insight. I'll never, ever forget it. "But we Your people, the sheep of Your pasture, will give thanks to You forever; from generation to generation we will recount Your praise" (Psalm 79:13).

Pastor means "shepherd." A Lutheran pastor is an *undershepherd*, carrying out a task and office that belongs to Jesus, "the great shepherd of the sheep." Jesus is the great pastoral example, the pastor par excellence. Yes, Jesus often speaks hard words when the Law is needed to bring repentance (Mark 8:33), but He does so in a context where "the good shepherd lays down his life for the sheep" (John 10:11). Love marks the life of Jesus and His undershepherds (John 3:16; 1 Timothy 4:12). A pastor forgives (John 20:23; 2 Corinthians 2:10). A pastor doles out the Lord's words and gifts (2 Timothy 4:2; 1 Corinthians 11:23). A pastor teaches with patience and kindness (1 Timothy 3:3; 1 Timothy 4:12ff.). A pastor serves (John 12:13ff.). A pastor prays for his people (2 Timothy 1:3). A pastor goes (Matthew 28:19). A pastor cares (Acts 6:1ff.). A pastor sacrifices (2 Corinthians 11:24ff.). A pastor is visible among his people (Mark 1:38). A pastor knows his people (John 10:14). A pastor sympathizes with his people and cares for and about his co-workers and parishioners (Romans 16:1–16). A pastor cares for those for whom his people care (Luke 8:41). A pastor suffers patiently, sometimes even at the hands of his sheep (2 Timothy 1:8ff.). A pastor is visible in his community (1 Timothy 3:7). A pastor spares no effort to bring back the wayward and find the lost (2 Timothy 4:5). A pastor seeks sheep "outside the fold" (John 10:16). A pastor leads with capable zeal (Romans 12:8). A pastor is aware of his own weaknesses and asks for forgiveness and patience (2 Corinthians 12:7ff.).

All this is a tall order; in fact, it is impossible. How could we pastors, "maggot sacks" of sin and weakness that we are (Luther), ever be up to this imitation of Christ and His apostles? Of ourselves, we cannot. But Christ, who gives the Office of the Holy Ministry, provides the grace sufficient for the task at hand.

In short, a pastor loves his people.

Love Your Pastor

"Obey your leaders and submit to them, for they are keeping watch over your souls, as those who will have to give an account. Let them do this with joy and not with groaning, for that would be of no advantage to you." (Hebrews 13:17)

Obey your leaders and submit to them . . ." What? In every-thing? In the color of the carpet in the parish hall? No. The reference is to submission to the clear Word of God. "Remember your teachers, those who spoke the word of God to you" (Hebrews 13:7). The pastor wears a stole. He's yoked, a man under authority. He's been placed in an office by Christ, through your congregation, not to make you happy. He's there to bring you joy—eternal joy through faith in the eternal Word of God. "Your words became to me a joy and the delight of my heart" (Jeremiah 15:16). That's a pastor's goal for all of us.

But we all have the sinful nature. So, when our pastor must speak the Law, we're prone to rebel, even become angry. "If it had not been for the law, I would not have known sin" (Romans 7:7). "Sorry, Carl! You and your girlfriend may be seventy years old, but shacking up is wrong. I don't care what the income tax rami-fications are!" Can you imagine the pressure, the burden a pastor bears, being the one who must "give an account" for the souls of his flock? On top of that, he has to deal with his own conscience (clearly knowing right from wrong) and face the ire of one man, one woman, a family or even a whole community for saying and doing what is right. No man should face this alone. But pastors often do. It can break a sensitive soul. It can sap his preaching. It can kill his prayer life. It can destroy his home life. It can drive him into loneliness and bring his visitation to a halt. It can cause him to vanish from the community.

What God gives, we receive, including the words and person of our faithful pastor. When the pastor is speaking and teaching in accord with the Word of God, his authority is God's—both to call sin what it is and to absolve (John 20:23). "He who hears you hears me" (Luke 10:16). This authority would seem oppressive or prone to abuse. And it can be and is—in its pseudo-forms. Jesus certainly did not "lord it over" anyone, and Paul followed Jesus in this regard. "Not that we lord it over your faith, but we work with you for your joy" (2 Corinthians 1:24). Peter gives pastors a specific pastoral admonition against coercion of the flock. "Shepherd the flock of God that is among you . . . not domineering over those in your charge, but being examples to the flock" (1 Peter 5:2–3).

Have you ever considered how frightening a task it is to know you must speak the Word of God whether folks like it or not? And then to do so as a sinful, emotional, fearful "maggot sack" (as Luther called himself) makes it a super-human burden. It's only possible to carry out the task with the help of Jesus and His grace (2 Timothy 1:6). Such a burden, combined with an eternally important responsibility, is enough to drive a man into loneliness and despair. But that's how Jesus became the Great Shepherd, and through crosses—and only through crosses—He continues to make great shepherds of fallible men (Galatians 6:14; 2 Corinthians 12:9). And through crosses, He also creates sheep ready to hear the voice of their shepherd and carry each other's burdens (including the pastor's).

Keep Us Sober and on the Horse

The world is like a drunken peasant. If one helps him into the saddle on one side, he will fall off on the other side.
—Martin Luther (Luther's Works, vol. 54, p. 111)

Sometimes the Church can be "like a drunken peasant" too. Jesus says, "The Son of Man came to seek and to save the lost" (Luke 19:10). This text comes at the end of the account of Jesus' visit to Zacchaeus's house. Zacchaeus was just the sort of unlikely character that Jesus sought out, and boy did the "religious experts" complain about it (v. 7). But Jesus declared, "Today salvation has come to this house, since he also is a son of Abraham. For the Son of Man came to seek and to save the lost" (vv. 9–10).

Luke's Gospel makes a particular, joyful emphasis on "the lost who are found." In the parable of the wedding feast (Luke 14:7–11), the "master" invites the guests to the great banquet. Those invited repeatedly come up with excuses, so the master commands that his servant go "to the highways and hedges and compel people to come in, that my house may be filled" (Luke 14:23). Then follows the sobering teaching: "Whoever does not bear his own cross and come after me cannot be my disciple" (Luke 14:27). And after that comes the parable of the lost sheep (Luke 15:1–7). The point? "There will be more joy in heaven over one sinner who repents than over ninety-nine righteous persons who need no repentance" (Luke 15:7). Next the woman finds the lost coin. "Rejoice with me, for I have found the coin that I had lost. Just so, I tell you, there is joy before the angels of God over one sinner who repents" (Luke 15:9–10). Then the parable of the prodigal son (Luke 15:11–32) with its fabulous conclusion: "This my son was dead, and is alive again; he was lost, and is found" (v. 24). Throughout all of these, who does the finding? It is certainly God the Father and also God the Son in these and many other texts.

How did Jesus in His earthly walk "seek the lost"? He went! He preached! He healed! He also appointed apostles ("sent ones"; Luke 9:1–6), and the Seventy-Two (Luke 10:1–12). The Book of Concord rightly states, "The office of the ministry [preaching office] stems from the general call of the apostles" (Treatise 10, German). But folks who encountered Jesus and who did not have a vocation as an apostle also had a tremendous hand in "seeking the lost." Think of the woman at the well. She went home, told others about Jesus, and "many Samaritans from that town believed in him because of the woman's testimony" (John 4:39). Or consider the Gerasene. After Jesus sent the demons named "Legion" into the swine, "the man from whom the demons had gone begged that he might be with him, but Jesus sent him away. . . . And he went away, proclaiming throughout the whole city how much Jesus had done for him" (Luke 8:38–39). These lives were radically changed by Jesus' Gospel, and they stayed in their communities, told others, and many believed.

Here's the "drunken peasant" part. We are prone to pit the glorious gift of the spiritual priesthood of all believers (with its right and privilege of speaking the Gospel in the context of everyday life) against the Office of the Ministry, which has the responsibility of serving at the behest of Christ through the call of a congregation. The former exists so "that you may proclaim the excellencies of him who called you out of darkness into his marvelous light" (1 Peter 2:9). All of us as spiritual priests have the right and responsibility to speak of Jesus to those in our lives and communities and to invite them to church! As pastors, some are given the responsibility of shepherding, proclaiming the Word, and giving the Sacraments to the gathered flock. Both activities are part of the mission of Jesus "to seek and to save the lost." When we pit these two offices or vocations against each other, we are on the wrong track.

To fall off one side of the horse is to say, "Laypeople don't have the right and responsibility of speaking the Gospel" or worse, "The Gospel is only effective when spoken by a pastor." To fall off the other side is to assert, "We don't need pastors. And men who are regularly preaching the Gospel and administering the Sacraments don't need to be pastors." Christ has given us both spiritual priests and pastors. That's His mission paradigm. When both are functioning as God has given, there is mutual love and complementary support.

God keep us sober . . . and on the horse!

Preaching Is All about "You"

We need to preach more about the Gospel!" a well-meaning pastor admonished his brothers at a pastoral conference. As he continued his speech, a little old man shuffled up to the microphone. It's hard to believe that this old pastor, barely over five feet tall, had been among the very first in all the German churches to reject publicly the Nazi platform and then struggled against Hitler for the rest of the war. He declared to his brother pastors: "For more than 50 years I have never preached *about* the Gospel. I have only *preached* the Gospel."

Hermann Sasse put his finger on a perennial weakness in our preaching. The sermon is not mere information. The preacher must dare to speak the biblical "you!" in both Law and Gospel. "*You* killed the Lord of glory." "*Your* righteous deeds are as filthy rags." "*You* are the man!" (Nathan to David).

And the Gospel is proclaimed the same way: "Today is born *for you* a Savior." "*Your* sins are forgiven." "*You* are raised with Him in Baptism." "The blood of Christ, shed for *you.*"

Preaching is a finger-pointing business. It takes courage to stand in the pulpit and let fly, accusing full-on with all the force of the damning Law. "The Law is to be preached in its full severity" (Walther). It takes more skill to preach the full and sweet Gospel to sinners accused. Yet the Bible is packed to the brim with Christ's full and free forgiveness, ready to be dished up and delivered by the lips of the preacher. "By killing he makes alive," Luther emphasized again and again. And so our preaching must kill the old man, damn him thoroughly to hell and raise him up again with Christ and His free forgiveness.

Preachers, let's sit at the feet of the apostles. Notice how many times "you" appears in Peter's sermon:

> Men of Israel . . . the God of Abraham, the God of Isaac, and the god of Jacob, the god of our fathers, glorified his servant Jesus, whom *you* delivered over and denied in the presence of Pilate, when he decided to release him. But *you* denied the Holy and Righteous One, and asked for a murderer to be granted to *you*, and *you* killed the Author of life, whom God raised from the dead. To this we are witnesses. . . . And now, brothers, I know that

you acted in ignorance, as did *your* rulers. But what God foretold by the mouth of all the prophets, that his Christ would suffer, he thus fulfilled. [*You*] repent therefore, and turn again, that *your* sins may be blotted out, that times of refreshing may come from the presence of the Lord, and that he may send the Christ appointed for *you*, Jesus, whom heaven must receive until the time for restoring all things about which God spoke by the mouth of his holy prophets long ago. Moses said, "The Lord God will raise up for *you* a prophet like me from *your* brothers. *You* shall listen to him in whatever he tells *you*. And it shall be that every soul who does not listen to that prophet shall be destroyed from the people." And all the prophets who have spoken, from Samuel and those who came after him, also proclaimed these days. *You* are the sons of the prophets and of the covenant that God made with *your* fathers, saying to Abraham, "And in *your* offspring shall all the families of the earth be blessed." God, having raised up his servant, sent him to *you* first, to bless *you* by turning everyone of *you* from y*our* wickedness. (Acts 3:12a, 13–15, 17–26)

I love a bit of humor in a sermon, a rhetorical surprise. A story is great, even the occasional personal story. I'm a fan of all sorts of styles, of changing things up and "finding a new string to thump" on occasion (Luther). But through it all, let's stop preaching limply and merely only about the Law and Gospel. Let's preach the Law in all its condemnation and the Gospel in its sweetness.

Back to Basics in Preaching

After his famous "Here I stand" speech before Emperor Charles V, Luther was "captured" by Prince Frederick and whisked away to hiding in the Wartburg castle. Meanwhile, things deteriorated back in Wittenberg—and badly. A fanatic took leadership of the church and forced changes upon people that were not in accord with the Gospel or the Scriptures. Luther hated coercion. The Gospel does not coerce. There were also some charismatics, called the "Zwickau Prophets," who came to town claiming the direct inspiration of the Holy Spirit. They claimed education wasn't needed to understand the Scriptures, so schools were closed, and maybe even the university! Luther resolved to return to his pulpit. On March 9, 1522, on Invocavit Sunday (First Sunday in Lent), Luther began preaching a series of eight sermons on these burning issues.

Go to *http://mercyjourney.blogspot.com/2013/02/luthers-invocavit-sermon-1522.html* to read Luther's first sermon of the series. My friends, the Lutheran Church was born of Luther's direct, profound but simple preaching style. He most often preached on Bible texts—the Sunday readings on Sundays and sermon series on whole books of the Bible or parts of the Bible during the week, line by line. He explained the Bible in a way that common people could understand it. Above all, Luther preached repentance and forgiveness in Christ. He was a master of Law-and-Gospel preaching. That's what the apostles preached (Acts 2–3).

I'd like you to read that very short sermon by Luther listed above, noting several things:

- The sermon is topical. It's on Christian patience, love and freedom.

- Note how often Luther references the Scriptures and what they teach.

- Note how he grabs the hearers' attention in the brief sermon introduction. "Everyone must fight his own battle with death by himself."

- Note how clearly he states the Law and the Gospel right up front in the first two paragraphs of the sermon.

- Note that in his third point, he makes a specific point of the Law. "Through love we must do to one another as God has done to us through faith."

- Note very carefully Luther's use of the pronouns "I," "you" and "we."

- Notice how Luther includes himself in Law statements and Gospel statements. "We are all the children of wrath."

- Notice how he uses "I" as he repeatedly expresses his intimate knowledge of his hearers, his love for them and his dismay at them: "I love you even as I love my own soul."

- Notice how he uses "you" and "we" to both preach very pointed Law and deliver the sweet Gospel.

As you read the sermon, you can visualize Luther looking directly at his hearers with his finger pointing at them. He did not rely on a manuscript. Luther preached from notes or simply by following the text of the Scriptures. Note, too, how he uses "you" in very pointed Law and Gospel statements. "A donkey can almost chant the lessons, and why shouldn't you be able to repeat the doctrines and formulas? . . . Faith without love is not enough." Note how direct and blunt Luther's language is. There's no guessing about his point.

That is a sermon calling the hearers to repentance and faith in Christ and teaching them what love and patience are. The sermon has a great deal of Law (to condemn and instruct). Later sermons in the week gave way to more Gospel. "But if you believe that God steps in for you and stakes all He has and His blood for you [in Christ] . . . then let us see what can harm you; come devil, death, sin, and hell and all creation" (AE 51:93).

Remember, that is a sermon in a dire circumstance calling for repentance. Other Luther sermons drip throughout with the sweetest delivery of the Gospel "for you." It's time for us to pay attention to the greatest preacher in history, aside from Jesus, John the Baptist and St. Paul. It's time for back-to-basics preaching.

A Letter to Pastors on Their Vocation of Serving

Dearest Brothers in the Office:

I greet you in the name of Jesus, our constant hope and consolation in the ministry.

I've been rereading Martin Brecht's great three-volume biography of Luther.* Luther's life was full of joy, love for the Scriptures, friendship, and great conviviality. But it was also filled with disappointment. Near the end of his life, he described himself as "old, cold, lame and one-eyed." He was so miffed at his own congregation in Wittenberg that the summer before he died, he resolved to leave town for good. He wrote Katie on July 28, 1545:

> I would like to arrange matters in such a way that I do not have to return to Wittenberg. My heart has become cold, so that I do not like to be there any longer. I wish you would sell the garden and field, house and all. . . . It would be best for you to move to Zölsdorf as long as I am still living and able to help you to improve the little property with my salary. . . . I would rather eat the bread of a beggar than torture and upset my poor old age and final days with the filth at Wittenberg, which destroys my hard and faithful work. You might inform Doctor Pomer and Master Philip of this (if you wish). (AE 50:278, 280–81)

Katie did inform them, and the Elector sent Melanchthon out with a reconnaissance party to retrieve the old man, promising to make some improvement in the city. Luther was indeed a grumpy old man by this time, but his frustrations with the congregations in Wittenberg were hardly limited to his old age. There was, of course, the uproar early on, while he was hiding in the Wartburg after his great "Here I stand" speech at Worms. (During this week of Invocavit, you might check out the first of Luther's "Invocavit Sermons" for a clinic on preaching to people in the pew, especially on preaching "love"; i.e., "third use of the Law!" See AE 51:70–75.) And already from 1526 to 1527 and the time of the plague in Wittenberg, Luther frequently expressed his great frustrations with the city parish, both in sermons and private correspondence. The Gospel did not have the effect among the people that he had hoped, and it bothered him greatly at times. Of course, as he readily admitted, his old sinful flesh only exacerbated the matter.

And so it is with us. One cannot paint the whole Missouri Synod ministerium with one broad brush, to be sure. There are many brothers experiencing excellent times in their lives of service at this moment, and abundantly so. There are also many experiencing the cross in their office, and intensely so. It is, in many respects, like the opening line of Charles Dickens' *A Tale of Two Cities*: "It was the best of times, it was the worst of times." It is a great moment in that, while postmodernity has demolished the purely rationalistic and empiricist opposition to metaphysical realities, leaving the door wide open for us to make the case for Jesus, yet the flood of "spirituality" and individualistic fantasy has pulled the populace away from the Church. Sadly, that includes a great many of our own. I don't need to rehearse here the demographic challenges that we, and all of Western Christianity, face. You know this challenge very directly and deal with it daily.

Brothers, there is consolation, even for ministers of the Gospel. "What God institutes and commands cannot be an empty thing. It must be a most precious thing, even though it looked like it had less value than a straw" (LC IV 8). Luther's comment applies to us pastors. "Therefore, every Christian has enough in Baptism to learn and to do all his life. For he has always enough to do by believing firmly what Baptism promises and brings: victory over death and the devil (Romans 6:3–6), forgiveness of sin (Acts 2:38), God's grace (Titus 3:5–6), the entire Christ, and the Holy Spirit with His gifts (1 Corinthians 6:11). In short, Baptism is so far beyond us that if timid nature could realize this, it might well doubt whether it could be true" (LC IV 41). Before you were called and ordained, all that is given in Baptism was yours. And it remains yours, even in times when your "timid nature" might not feel it or realize it.

And there is an even greater consolation precisely in your eternal election to salvation, which was made manifest in your Baptism. You know full well, pastor, all of those "in Him," "in Christ," "in the Beloved" statements in Ephesians 1. "In him you also, when you heard the Word of truth, the Gospel of your salvation, and believed in him, were sealed with the promised Holy Spirit, who is the guarantee of our inheritance until we acquire possession of it, to the praise of his glory" (v. 13). "In him we have redemption through his blood, the forgiveness of our trespasses, according to the riches of his grace, which he lavished upon us . . . making known to us the mystery of his will" (vv. 7f.). You are baptized, pastor. That rock won't move, come what may.

Moreover, you have not chosen your vocation by yourself. Sure, God gave you a desire to study for the ministry (1 Timothy 3:1); you were encouraged along the way by God's people. Faithful teachers encouraged you. But it was the church which finally put you into an office, or *Amt* (auf Deutsch). "St. Paul tells Timothy and Titus to entrust the ministry to faithful and able men (2 Tim. 2:2; 3:2; Titus 1:9)" (Chemnitz, *Enchiridion*, 28**). The church recognized your gifts, and God's people in a specific location called you with a "special and legitimate" call. You were prepared, called, and ordained to this ministry; you didn't just start "gassing off" on your own (Romans 10:15; Jeremiah 23:21; Hebrews 5:4).

It is certainly true that all Christians are spiritual priests and enjoy the full privileges of this priesthood. As Chemnitz wrote, "All Christians have a general call to proclaim the Gospel of God (Rom. 10:9); to speak the Word of God among themselves (Eph. 5:19); to admonish each other from the Word of God; to reprove (Eph. 5:11; Matt. 19:15) and to comfort (1 Thess. 4:18). And family heads are enjoined to do this with the special command that they give their households the instruction of the Lord (Eph. 6:4). But the public ministry of the Word and of the Sacraments in the Church is not entrusted to all Christians in general, as we have already shown (1 Cor. 12:28; Eph. 4:12). For a special or particular call is required for this (Romans 10:15)" (Chemnitz, *Enchiridion*, 29).

I've always loved being a pastor. There is something amazing about being invited into people's lives at their very best times and very worst times, and often in the lives of the very same people! But much more than that, we come into the lives of people with Jesus. It's all about Jesus. It's all about Jesus for those who already know Him, and it's all about Jesus for those who don't. And as Dr. Walther so concisely and wonderfully stated in Thesis III of *The Church and the Office of the Ministry*, "The preaching office is not an optional office but one whose establishment has been commanded to the Church and to which the Church is properly bound till the end of time" (*Church and Office*, 181;*** Walther's proof-text for this is Matthew 28:19–20). The office is not finally about power or even authority in the sense that we usually think of. Jesus, after all, exercised His authority (*exousia*) by sacrificing Himself (Philippians 2). Thus, as Walther states (Thesis IV): "The preaching office [*Predigtamt*] is not a special state in opposition to or holier than that of ordinary Christians, as was the Levitical priesthood; rather it is an office of service [*Amt des Dienstes*]." And we pastors are called to serve up Jesus. "We preach Christ crucified," or we should not speak at all, frankly. We bring the love of Jesus to the hurting, the weak, the sick, the destitute, the lonely, the aged, the young, and everyone in between. And we do so because the Lord mandates that there be pastors after His own heart who do so.

Chemnitz notes several reasons why a pastor must have a legitimate call, and these points provide consolation for us today. It is not merely a matter of human arrangement or good order, he says.

1. "God himself deals with us in the church through the ministry as through the ordinary means and instrument. For it is He Himself that speaks, exhorts, absolves, baptizes, etc., in the ministry and through the ministry (Luke 1:70; Heb. 1:1; John 1:23; 2 Cor. 2:10, 17; 5:20; 13:3)." So, states Chemnitz, we have clear proofs that God wants to use pastors as "His ordinary means and instrument." If God is so minded, will He not hear your prayers, Pastor? Does He not care for you too?

2. "Very many and necessary gifts are required for the ministry (2 Cor. 2:16). But one who has been brought to the ministry by a legitimate call can apply the divine promises to himself, ask God for faithfulness in them, and expect both, the gifts that are necessary for him rightly to administer the ministry (1 Tim. 4:14; 2 Tim. 1:6; 2 Cor. 3:5–6) and governance and protection in the office entrusted to him (Is. 49:2; 51:16)."

3. "The chief thing of the ministry is that God wants to be present in it with His Spirit, grace and gifts and to work effectively through it. But Paul says in Romans 10:15: 'How shall they who are not sent preach' (namely in such a way that faith is engendered by hearing)? But God wants to give increase to the planting and watering of those who have been legitimately called to

the ministry and set forth doctrine without guile and faithfully administer whatever belongs to the ministry (1 Cor. 3:6; 15:58), that both they themselves and others might be saved (1 Tim. 4:16)."

4. "The assurance of a divine call stirs up minsters of the Word, that each one, in his station, in the fear of God, performs his functions with greater diligence, faith and eagerness, without weariness. And he does not let himself be drawn or frightened away from his office by fear of any peril or of persecution, since he is sure that he is called by God and that the office has been divinely entrusted to him."

5. "Finally, on this basis the hearers are stirred up to true reverence and obedience toward the ministry, namely since they are taught from the Word of God that God, present through this means, wants to deal with us in the church and work effectively among us" (Chemnitz, *Enchiridion*, 29–30).

Dear Brothers in the office, we have a sacred vocation of service. We serve. Because we bear Christ's own office, an office our Confessions say is derived from Christ and the apostles, we can expect among the joys and great blessings, thorns, trials, crosses, and difficulties. Some of these are brought upon us by the weaknesses of those whom we serve. But the office is an office designed *only* to serve sinners! This is the way of Christ. Some difficulties, often more than we might like to admit, we bring upon ourselves through our own weaknesses and sinfulness. And I think, especially in my own life, of my sins of discontentment and anxiety. Yet we know, in repentance, that even our own failings are worked for good by our merciful heavenly Father!

I covet your prayers, even as I pledge you mine. I plan to write these letters from time to time to encourage you, not to burden you.

---

*Martin Brecht, *Martin Luther,* trans. James L. Schaaf, 3 vols. (Minneapolis: Fortress, 1985–93).

**Martin Chemnitz, *Ministry, Word, and Sacraments: An Enchiridion,* trans. Luther Poellot (St. Louis: Concordia Publishing House, 1981).

*** C. F. W. Walther, *The Church and the Office of the Ministry,* trans. Matthew C. Harrison (St. Louis: Concordia Publishing House, 2012).

Christ and the Church

What does *koinonia* mean when members of the fellowship are in need? "All who believed were together and had all things in common [*ta koina*]. And they were selling their possessions and belongings and distributing the proceeds to all, as any had need" (Acts 2:44–45). "There was not a needy person among them" (4:34). The fellowship of believers acted in Acts 6 to meet the need of the Greek-speaking Jewish widows being overlooked in the daily *diakonia,* or distribution, of food. It was the formal beginning to the Church's intentional, ordered life of mercy. It is also the beginning of what is popularly called "stewardship."

Paul was converted in AD 36, just after the martyrdom of Stephen. (For more on New Testament dates, check out Bo Reicke's *Re-examining Paul's Letters: The History of the Pauline Correspondence.*) By AD 45–46, he was in Syrian Antioch (11:25–26). The Christians in Antioch decided "to send relief [*diakonia*] to the brothers living in Judea" (11:29). The persecution and martyrdom continued, and refugees fleeing Jerusalem for Antioch kept the latter well-informed. The general famine announced by Agabus must have hit the already persecuted Christians in Jerusalem with intensity. Fields were fallow in AD 47 in Palestine because of a Sabbath year, which made the situation all the worse.

It is significant that the first account of the proclamation of the Gospel in Acts to Gentiles coincides (11:20) with the first collection. The collection for the poor is born at the rough edge of the Church's mission to the Gentiles. Mercy and mission go hand in hand. Where there is Christ, there is the Church (Ignatius, "To the Smyrnaeans," 8.2). Loehe said that "mission is nothing but the one church of God in motion" (CTS Press's *Three Books about the Church*). Where the Church is in motion, there is mission, mercy, and money.

The controversy over Gentile converts and what to do about circumcision grew quickly until the Apostolic Council of Acts 15 dealt with the issue definitively. The apostle describes the resolution to the circumcision controversy: "And when James and Cephas and John, who seemed to be pillars, perceived the grace that was given to me, they gave the right hand of fellowship [*koinonia*] to Barnabas and me, that we should go to the Gentiles and they to the circumcised. Only, they asked us to remember the poor, the very thing I was eager to do" (Galatians 2:9–10).

Paul went to the Gentiles and demonstrated that he was "eager" to remember the poor. For Paul, fellowship is doctrinal agreement with ethical ramifications, with a focus on care for the needy. *Koinonia* is vertical and horizontal. St. Paul took this fellowship (collection) so seriously that it occupied him for over a decade.

The collection was the reason for this last trip to Jerusalem (Romans 15:28). Paul's life was put on the path to Rome and eventually martyrdom because he was apprehended while delivering the collection for the poor (Acts 24:17); 2 Corinthians 8 and 9 are Paul's great explanation of the collection. In those chapters, he works to convince the wealthy Corinthian Christian community to give generously. It is from these two chapters that many of the popular stewardship texts come. Read some of them: 8:5, 7, 9, 12, 14; 9:6, 7, 10–11.

This list of texts should cause one to pause. The primary reason for giving money in the New Testament is for poor and suffering Christians. The giving begins with Christ giving of Himself unto death for our sins. Giving is also a demonstration of fellowship. St. Paul spent well over a decade of his working life organizing, arranging, leading, and bringing to a conclusion the great collection for the poor in Jerusalem. Is this what takes place in the Church today?

Let's Hear It for the Small Congregation!

Amid all the hype in The Lutheran Church—Missouri Synod over the last number of years about "growth," some important facts about small congregations have been overlooked. In fact, I wouldn't be surprised that "if such a thing were measurable," all the well-meant talk about getting congregations to grow has in many cases impeded the very numerical growth we all want.

What do I mean? I'm afraid that much of the material that we "Synod types" have put out in the church in this regard, while well-intentioned and often very good advice, has disregarded the great blessings Jesus brings people in the small congregation. When our talk is all about "grow, grow, growth, mega, meta, magnificent," we run the very strong risk of giving "inadvertently" the small parish the message "You're bad, you're sick; you're backward, you're abnormal." Any pastor worth his salt, with a decade or two of experience under his belt, will tell you that one significant factor in whether or not a church grows is how its members view their parish. That was certainly my experience in the parish.

I'd like to put before you a few simple thoughts in order to affirm and build up our small churches. Of the some 6,150 LCMS churches around the nation, 73 percent (4,510, almost three-fourths!) have fewer than 500 members on their rolls; 38 percent have fewer than 200 members; 35 percent have between 200 and 500 members. Of those parishes of 200 or fewer members, average attendance is 53. For those between 200 and 500 members, average Sunday attendance is 128. Yet nearly one-third of these small parishes operate schools! That, frankly, is amazing!

Here are a couple more interesting stats. We know that as a percentage of the congregational budget, small congregations give considerably more to their district and to the Synod. And perhaps as significant as anything, smaller congregations have in many cases significantly better member attendance (48 percent attendance for the 2,363 churches under 200 members).

Over the course of my pastoral service, I served two parishes. (One was well above 500 members; the other somewhat below that number.) I can tell you from experience, the quality of pastoral care in smaller congregations is quite often phenomenal. The LCMS has some of the best-trained clergy in the nation. The vast majority of our pastors and teachers serve parishes with small numbers with "full-scale" commitment. This blessing has marked the existence of our Synod from her earliest days and will continue to mark our existence well into the future. Despite radically changing demographics, many rural parishes live out their lives in Christ with "gusto."

Are there challenges and areas in which we fall short? Of course. But this little article is about the good things.

More important than anything else is that in these small parishes, Christ Himself, through His blessed Word and Sacrament, dwells to give sinners life and salvation. That is a point C. F. W. Walther loved to drive home when he sensed any devaluation of smaller parishes by anyone in the Synod. Very important to me as President of the LCMS is that so many small parishes so well approximate the ideal Luther held up for the church, as we all are members of the same body, caring for one another. He spoke about the Lord's Supper:

> Christ said, I am the head, I will first give Myself
> for you, will make your suffering and misfortune
> Mine own and bear it for you, that you in your
> turn may do the same for Me and for one anoth-
> er, have all things in common in Me and with me,
> and let this sacrament be unto you a sure token
> of that all, that you may not forget me. (*On the
> Blessed Sacrament*, 1519)

Christ cares for us, gives Himself for us. We in turn give ourselves for the neighbor. This happens nowhere as well, as naturally, and as constantly as in the small parish. Where mistakes are made, we flee to the forgiving waters of Baptism, confess our sins, and resolve in faith to begin anew in love, both "laying down our burdens in the midst of the congregation" (Luther) and also finding the burdens of others there to take up. God knows that as we often know well the sins of our neighbors (and they know ours!) in smaller congregations, the need for forgiveness and grace as we work together is all the greater!

We heartily support, thank God for, and affirm our many larger congregations that have been blessed by circumstances, God-given wisdom, demographics, and grace to work hard, all which have allowed them to grow to such an extent. But let us always give thanks for the small congregations, which constantly remind us all that the church on earth is truly, and always, a "little flock."

Come to think of it, the Synod would do best if we had many, many more small congregations!

Music in Service of the Gospel

Some of Luther's most famous accolades for music came in a preface he wrote to musician Georg Rhau's *Delightful Symphonies* (1538). "Next to the Word of God, music deserves the highest praise. . . . Whether you wish to comfort the sad, to terrify the happy, to encourage the despairing, to humble the proud, to calm the passionate, or to appease those full of hate . . . what more effective means than music could you find?" Those unaffected by the delights of music as a bearer of the Word of God "deserve to hear . . . the music of the pigs."

Luther concludes his preface with a few sentences that could have been written yesterday: "Let this noble, wholesome, and cheerful creation of God be commended to you. By it you may escape shameful desires and bad company. At the same time you may by this creation accustom yourself to recognize and praise the Creator. Take special care to shun perverted minds who prostitute this lovely gift of nature and of art with their erotic rantings; and be quite assured that none but the devil goads them on to defy their very nature which would and should praise God its Maker with this gift, so that these [colorful word deleted] purloin the gift of God and use it to worship the foe of God, the enemy of nature and of this lovely art" (Luther's Works, vol. 53, pp. 323–24).

The hymnals of Luther's day contained orders and resources for services and prayers, along with hymns. In fact, it was the Lutheran Reformation, riding on the wave of Gutenberg's press, that brought forth hymnals. And they've been a hit ever since.

Some years ago, as the LCMS was working toward a new hymnal, the naysayers commented: "Well, you're going to have a whole warehouse full of those things." Even in this digital age, *Lutheran Service Book* (*LSB*) has far outperformed *Lutheran Worship* (1982), which peaked at only a 56 percent penetration among LCMS congregations. Today, *LSB* is used in nearly 90 percent of the Synod's congregations. Its electronic version, *Lutheran Service Builder*, is used widely to assist congregations in printing bulletins. *LSB* is certainly one of the best-selling books in the history of Concordia Publishing House, with more than one million copies in print.

Luther applied his thoughts on Christian freedom to the matter of worship. Under the Gospel, "a Christian is a perfectly free lord of all, subject to none." Under the law of love, "a Christian is a perfectly dutiful servant of all, subject to all" (Luther's Works, vol. 31, p. 344). There is unbelievable freedom in worship (Galatians 5:1). Yet, as St. Paul teaches, we are to use our freedom in service to our neighbor, and we therefore accept limits to our freedom (Galatians 5:13).

It would be irksome or even offensive for everyone to have completely different worship practices and forms every week, though it would not necessarily be sinful. Many would find it irksome and tiring to have no variety in the weekly service. The hymnal allows both stability and variety. To be sure, the freedom we have stretches beyond using the hymnal, so long as what is done in song and liturgy does not confound the Gospel and detract from Christ. We do say, however, that the order of the service should be followed. At the least, the parts of the service should be present. Why? They hold up Christ and deliver the Gospel. We should not omit a clear confession of sins by the people and absolution by the pastor. We should not ditch the readings. We should and must preach textual sermons, with clear Law and Gospel applied directly to those present. The Lord's Supper should follow confession and preaching as preparation. We should not be messing with the Lord's Words of Institution. We are to be responsible in distributing the Sacrament to those who confess that the body and blood are present and who are in confessional fellowship with us (see Explanation of the Small Catechism, especially Question 305). Exceptions are exceptions, not the rule.

Witness and Mission

The Worldwide Reach of the Gospel

"He [Jesus] had compassion for them, because they were harassed and helpless, like sheep without a shepherd. Then he said to his disciples, 'The harvest is plentiful, but the laborers are few; therefore pray earnestly to the Lord of the harvest to send out laborers into his harvest.'" (Matthew 9:36–38)

No institution or human factor of the LCMS has been more significant in the spread of the pure Gospel of Jesus and His grace than our two seminaries. Most of us, when considering the work of the St. Louis and Fort Wayne seminaries, have the domestic scene in mind. Many LCMS people think of the seminaries only when it's time to call a graduate. And that is significant in its own right!

But the seminaries are a resource for the worldwide spread of the Gospel and the strengthening of the Lutheran Church around the globe. This happens through the training of missionaries and in the training of students from around the world. It is critical that both seminaries retain strong residential master of divinity programs. These are the foundations that also allow for strong graduate-studies programs. For decades, students from all over the world have come to study at our schools. They have returned vastly strengthened in knowledge and passion for the Gospel and have had a profound effect upon churches worldwide.

There is a moment of opportunity that is opening wide before us. The Lord is answering our prayer: "Pray the Lord of the harvest sends workers." And He's answering it in a very significant way. There is no other Lutheran church body in the world that combines fidelity to the Gospel and all its articles as confessed in the Book of Concord with the remarkable capacity and worldwide reach of the LCMS.

It is time to increase vastly the number of international students at our seminaries, not just students studying to become pastors but pastors who are church leaders and future leaders, professors and seminary instructors, in short, the future leaders of world Lutheranism.

Great, solid, Lutheran education that is completely committed to the inerrant Scriptures and the teachings of Luther are the gift and vocation of the LCMS. Our seminaries have been doing this for decades and very successfully too! It's time to provide this opportunity for many more around the world. Funding this effort is an aid to domestic students because tuition assistance keeps costs lower for all students. Having our students rub shoulders with international students opens their eyes to mission opportunities at home and around the world.

> If we therefore want to show true mercy to the world and to those around us, doing the most important work of Christian mercy, then we must educate and send out teachers of the Gospel. That is also taught in our text. Our text reports that while Christ taught, He also healed all sorts of illness among the people. But when He sums up the desperate situation of the people and places it before our eyes, He does not say, "Pray to the Lord for doctors." He says rather, "Pray to the Lord that He send workers," that is, teachers and preachers, "into His harvest." It is not that the Christian should not be merciful also over against physical need, but rather because He desires to emphasize that they do the most important work of Christian mercy in the preparation and sending out of teachers of the Gospel. (Francis Pieper)

Before God and to the World

The Lutheran Reformation had been in full swing for nearly six years, but Martin Luther had yet to write his first hymn. A profound event moved his poetic and musical soul. Within a short period following, most of the hymns and liturgies he produced during his lifetime would gush forth in a flood of firm conviction and deep faith in Christ. What was the event?

Two young men, Augustinian brothers like Luther, were burned at the stake in Brussels on July 1, 1523, for preaching the Gospel of free forgiveness in Christ. They were the first martyrs of the Lutheran Reformation. Luther wrote a hymn in the popular ballad form of the day. Used by the town criers of his day to deliver the latest news from village to village, Luther's use of the ballad form spread the news of these martyrs' deaths, as well as the precious Gospel for which they died.

> The first right fitly John was named,
> So rich he in God's favor;
> His brother, Henry—one unblamed,
> Whose salt lost not its savor.
>
> From this world they are gone away,
> The diadem they've gained;
> Honest, like God's good children, they
> For his word life disdained,
> And have become his martyrs.
> (Luther's Works 53:214)

The familiar term *martyr* comes from a Greek New Testament word often translated "witness." In its simplest (legal) use, a witness is merely one who recounts the facts observed (Matthew 18:16). Thus, it was crucial for the place of Judas among the Twelve to be filled with "a witness of the resurrection" (Acts 1:22), since the apostolic band was told by the risen Christ, "You shall be my witnesses . . . to the ends of the earth" (Acts 1:8). John's Gospel and letters show a particular interest in such "bearing witness" (*martyria*)—an understandable fact since John was writing late in the first century as the eyewitnesses to the events surrounding Jesus were quickly passing into eternity.

Of John the Baptizer, the text says, "And there came a man sent from God by the name of John. This one came as a witness (*martyrian*) . . . that all might believe through him" (John 1:7). The text of John 1 is worth a careful read. What is John's testimony of Jesus? "This is the witness (*martyria*) of John. . . . He confessed and did not deny, and he confessed, 'I am not the Christ'" (John 1:19–20). John called for repentance (John 1:23) and then pointed to Jesus with a witness so profound it has been repeated in the liturgy of the Church since at least the seventh century: "Behold, the Lamb of God who takes away the sin of the world" (John 1:29). Finally, like Jesus, John the Baptizer sealed that witness with his own blood. How many faithful Christians have been safely guided to Jesus by John's witness? Countless millions.

The greatest witness, however, is not John, but Jesus Himself. Paul bids Timothy to "fight the good fight of faith, take hold of the eternal life for which you were called when you confessed the good confession before many witnesses." For, as Paul continues, "Jesus Christ himself bore witness to Pontius Pilate in the good confession" (1 Timothy 6:12, 13).

Today the fundamental gift and task of the Lutheran Church is to bear witness to Jesus Christ—to His Gospel and all its facets (AC VII 2; FC Ep X 7). This is our task toward each other. This is our task over against those who do not know Jesus. This is also the sacred vocation and ecumenical task of the Missouri Synod to world Christianity. We exist to bear witness—even to the point of suffering and death (and it may well come to that sooner than later here in the West)—to salvation by grace alone, through faith alone, on account of Christ alone. This Gospel is God's own testimony about Himself. This is the very confession of Christ Himself. This is the witness of the apostolic Church and the Church of all ages. This is the witness sealed by the blood of Jesus, the blood of John the Baptizer, and the burning of John and Henry, confessed and sung by Luther.

"Therefore, since we are surrounded by so great a cloud of witnesses [such as Brothers John and Henry, Luther, John the Baptist, and especially Christ] . . . let us run with endurance the race that is set before us" (Hebrews 12:1).

Confession or Witness?

I t's no secret that we in the Missouri Synod struggle to live in the unity that Christ so freely and generously gives us in His blessed Gospel of salvation by faith in the cross alone.

A significant "fault line" that has divided us is whether the Church's primary task is either *witness* or *confession*. Shall we be primarily *witnesses* of the Gospel or *confessors* of truth? The Synod creaks and groans and undergoes occasional tectonic shifts relative to these issues.

In fact, these tensions have been with us since the very beginning and are, in a way, represented by the two major streams of Lutheranism (Loehe and Walther), which were melded into one Synod. The seismic synodical divide is full of crags and cliffs— misunderstandings, assumptions, prejudices, and presumptions. Each viewpoint represents more than a bit of the truth.

On the *witness* side of the fault, the primary, laudable, and biblical goal is reaching the lost—now, in today's world, in a way people today can actually hear it. "I have become all things to all people, that by all means I might save some" (1 Corinthians 9:22). "For the Son of Man came to seek and to save the lost" (Luke 19:10).

Meanwhile, those who are convinced that the fundamental aspect of the Church's life in this world is *confession*—that is, holding forth for the truth of the Gospel and all its articles— rightly and intensely identify with New Testament texts that bid us to stand fast against world, culture and prevailing trends. "Let us hold fast the confession of our hope without wavering, for he who promised is faithful" (Hebrews 10:23). "That faith, however, that does not present itself in confession is not firm" (Ap IV 385).

These two great truths of the Christian life are represented by two powerful and pervasive New Testament words: *martyria*, or *witness*, and *homologia*, or *confession*. *Witness* is used in the New Testament for a straightforward witness to facts (Matthew 18:16). The apostolic circle were witness to the resurrection in the legal sense, that is, they actually saw the risen Christ. As such, they were commissioned by Christ Himself to "bear witness" to what they had seen and heard (Matthew 10:18), and such witness produced faith in others.

So right from Pentecost, the *witness* becomes more than just a dispassionate reciting of historical fact. To be a witness was now to speak with faith and conviction about what God had done and continues to do in Jesus: to save people from their sins. In the second century, there arose the common use of *witness* as *martyr* for a Christian who has been murdered for the faith. It is clearly the intent of Jesus that the Church bear witness through all time to His saving Gospel; that is at the essence of her very being and life (Luke 21:13; Isaiah 44:8; Acts 1:8).

To my great surprise and delight, while studying and paging through my Greek New Testament, I came upon a truth which is, I believe, vital for us as we seek to live together as a church. I discovered that in the New Testament, *witness* and *confession* belong together.

Finally the witness is given by the disciples themselves (Jn. 1:27; 1 Jn. 4:14). Their witness is confession. "Witness" (*Marturein*) and "confession" (*homologein*) merge into one another (1 Jn. 4:14ff)" [Kittel, *Theological Dictionary of the New Testament*, 4:498].

I've come to be convinced by the Bible that *witness* requires the strong confession of the truth as it is in Jesus—"teaching all things which I have commanded you" (Matthew 28:19); "the doctrine and all its articles" (FC SD X 31). Likewise, *confession* ("Here I stand!") that does not "Go, therefore, into all nations" is not the full confession of Jesus. Put simply, witness without confession is not witness. And confession without witness is not confession.

Confession or witness? Yes! God grant us such a life together.

Church and State

Genius and Courage

Late in 1821, Rev. Frederick Schaeffer presided over the cornerstone laying of a new building for the Evangelical Lutheran Church of St. Matthew in New York City. Afterward, he sent his homily to James Madison, the "father of the US Constitution" and chief author of the Bill of Rights.

Pastor Schaeffer's address was rather strongly Lutheran, in spite of the general weakness of American Lutheranism prior to 1840. Madison replied:

Montpellier, Dec. 3rd, 1821

Revd Sir,—I have received, with your letter of November 19th, the copy of your address at the ceremonial of laying the corner-stone of St Matthew's Church in New York.

It is a pleasing and persuasive example of pious zeal, united with pure benevolence and of a cordial attachment to a particular creed, untinctured with sectarian illiberality. It illustrates the excellence of a system which, by a due distinction, to which the genius and courage of Luther led the way, between what is due to Caesar and what is due God, best promotes the discharge of both obligations. The experience of the United States is a happy disproof of the error so long rooted in the unenlightened minds of well-meaning Christians, as well as in the corrupt hearts of persecuting usurpers, that without a legal incorporation of religious and civil polity, neither could be supported. A mutual independence is found most friendly to practical Religion, to social harmony, and to political prosperity.

In return for your kind sentiments, I tender assurances of my esteem and my best wishes.

James Madison

Schaeffer had struck several notes that resonated with Madison, so much so that the aging former president and constitutional patriarch noted "a due distinction, to which the genius and courage of Luther led the way, between what is due to Caesar and what is due God, [that] best promotes the discharge of both obligations." Wow. The drafter of the Bill of Rights, including the First Amendment ("Congress shall make no law respecting an establishment of religion, or prohibiting the free exercise thereof"), wrote, "The genius and courage of Luther led the way."

What is the "due distinction . . . between what is due to Caesar and what is due God"? This is a reference to Luther's two kingdoms doctrine. Historic, pre-Reformation Catholicism perpetuated the myth of the "Donation of Constantine"—that the Emperor Constantine (ca. AD 317) had given authority to the papacy to rule the Roman Empire, and that the Church was supposedly given the divine right and authority to govern both itself and the world. This was used to justify all sorts of mischief through the centuries following, where the Church meddled in governmental affairs and vice versa.

A second approach emerged at the time of the Reformation among the so-called radical reformers. They asserted that society should be ruled only by the Bible. This either led to a radical withdrawal from participation in civil society (e.g., the Amish) or to the view that a "Christian government" is needed to institute biblical principles upon society (e.g., the Puritans and their legacy). The views of both the Roman Catholics as well as the radical reformers resulted in a "mixing the kingdoms."

Luther's view, however, is unique. In view of texts like "The truth will set you free" (John 8:32) and "Render unto Caesar what is Caesar's and unto God what is God's" (Matthew 22:21, author's translation), Luther asserted that the conscience, the religious convictions of the individual Christian, belongs to God and not the government. The Bible teaches two distinct realms.

The "right hand" realm or kingdom is that of the Church. In this kingdom, there is to be no coercion, no force, no corporal punishment. It is a kingdom ruled solely by the Word of God in service to the Gospel of Christ. "My kingdom is not of this world" (John 18:36). It is a kingdom whose glory is hidden in weakness, small numbers, persecution, reviling and the like— makes no sense to reason whatsoever things like "the resurrection of the body," "baptismal regeneration," or "the body and blood of Christ" in the Lord's Supper.

The "left hand" kingdom is temporal government. This kingdom, too, is established by God (Romans 13:1–7). It flows from the Fourth Commandment ("Honor your father and your mother"). This kingdom operates not by revelation but by reason or natural law. The Gentiles, "when they do the things of the law, demonstrate that the law is written on their hearts" (Romans 2:14, author's translation). The governing authorities do "not bear the sword in vain" (Romans 13:4). Temporal government is established by God for maintaining good order, for peace, and to thwart evil (by just war and other means). When government forbids the Gospel, however, or commands us to act against a Christian conscience informed by the inerrant Word of God, then "we must obey God rather than men" (Acts 5:29).

When natural law or reason is functioning properly, it agrees with the Ten Commandments. In fact, the law "written on the heart" is the point of contact with the Law revealed in the Ten Commandments. That's why the preaching of the Law hits home with people who don't know Christ. God designed it that way as preparation for the Gospel! When it is commonly said that America was founded as a "Christian nation," that is only true in the sense that the overwhelming number of the founders were Christians, and that they recognized the benefit Christianity affords government.

Our founders recognized that "Christian morality" agreed with reason and natural law (law evident to any reasonable person). What was new in America was that there was no nationally established church or religion. But from the beginning, the national government was favorably oriented toward religion and acted to promote it. Even Jefferson (who moved from Deism to Unitarianism) went to church every Sunday of his presidency at Christian services held in the House Chambers! Offering government facilities today for services would be viewed by many secularists and courts as a gross violation of the "separation of church and state." Yet, there are dozens of such examples of our founders recognizing the great blessing of religion. For the government to thwart religion—so far as it contributes to morality and peace (and this is why orthodox Islam is problematic)—is foolish and self-destructive.

As James Madison indicated to Pastor Schaeffer, our founders had a view of the relationship of church and state that was much closer to Luther than to that of modern secularists. The Church serves the state by providing moral, charitable and decent people. The state serves the Church by providing peace and order, a context in which religious ends may prosper. The state is not to legislate matters of religious conscience. The church is not to meddle in the affairs of the state, nor is it to expect the state to operate according to anything other than sound reason.

"Luther rendered greater services to mankind. . . . At present it is more extensively admitted than formerly that no religious or political institution can be salutary and prosperous, unless it is established on the principles for which he become the successful champion."

I agree with Pastor Schaeffer . . . and James Madison.

I Will Speak before Kings, O God …

On February 16, 2012, President Harrison gave the following statement before the US House of Representatives Committee on Government Oversight.

Mr. Chairman, it's a pleasure to be here. The Lutheran Church—Missouri Synod is a body of some 6,200 congregations and 2.3 million members across the US. We don't distribute voters' lists. We don't have a Washington office. We are studiously nonpartisan, so much so that we're often criticized for being quietistic.

I'd rather not be here, frankly. Our task is to proclaim, in the words of the blessed apostle St. John, that the blood of Jesus Christ, God's Son, cleanses us from all our sin. And we care for the needy. We haven't the slightest intent to Christianize the government. Martin Luther famously quipped one time, "I'd rather have a smart Turk than a stupid Christian governing me."

We confess that there are two realms, the church and the state. They shouldn't be mixed—the church is governed by the Word of God, the state by natural law and reason, the Constitution.

We have 1,000 grade schools and high schools, 1,300 early childhood centers, 10 colleges and universities. We are a machine that produces good citizens for this country, and at tremendous personal cost.

We have the nation's only historic black Lutheran college in Concordia, Selma. Many of our people [who are alive today] walked with Dr. King fifty years ago on the march from Selma to Montgomery. We put up the first million dollars and have continued to provide finance for the Nehemiah Project in New York, as it has continued over the years, to provide home ownership for thousands of families, many of them headed by single women. Our agency in New Orleans, Camp Restore, rebuilt over 4,000 homes after Katrina, through the blood, sweat, and tears of our volunteers. Our Lutheran Malaria Initiative, barely begun, has touched the lives of 1.6 million people in East Africa, especially those affected by disease—women and children. And this is just the tip, the very tip, of the charitable iceberg.

I'm here to express our deepest distress over the HHS provisions. We are religiously opposed to supporting abortion-causing drugs. That is, in part, why we maintain our own health plan. While we are grandfathered under the very narrow provisions of the HHS policy, we are deeply concerned that our consciences may soon be martyred by a few strokes on the keyboard as this administration moves us all into a single-payer . . . system. Our direct experience in the *Hosanna-Tabor* case with one of our congregations gives us no comfort that this administration will be concerned to guard our free-exercise rights.

We self-insure 50,000 people. We do it well. Our workers make an average of $43,000 a year; 17,000 teachers make much less, on average. Our health plan was preparing to take significant cost-saving measures, to be passed on to our workers, just as this health-care legislation was passed. We elected not to make those changes, incur great cost, lest we fall out of the narrow provisions required under the grandfather clause. While we are opposed in principle not to all forms of birth control but only abortion-causing drugs, we stand with our friends in the Catholic Church and all others, Christians and non-Christians, under the free exercise and conscience provisions of the US Constitution.

Religious people determine what violates their consciences, not the federal government. The conscience is a sacred thing. Our church exists because overzealous governments in northern Europe made decisions that trampled the religious convictions of our forebearers. I have ancestors who served in the Revolutionary War. I have ancestors who were on the Lewis and Clark expedition. I have ancestors who served in the War of 1812, who fought for the North in the Civil War—my 88-year-old father-in-law has recounted to me, in tears many times, the horrors of the Battle of the Bulge. In fact, Bud Day, the most highly decorated veteran alive, is a member of The Lutheran Church—Missouri Synod. [Note: Bud Day was called home to heaven in 2013.]

We fought for a free conscience in this country, and we won't give it up without a fight. To paraphrase Martin Luther, the heart and conscience has room only for God, not for God and the federal government. The bed is too narrow, the blanket is too short. We must obey God rather than men, and we will. Please get the federal government, Mr. Chairman, out of our consciences. Thank you.

God Works for All Good

Christians . . . are able to swallow and devour whatever evils confront them and confidently to expect a thousand advantages for one disadvantage or loss." Thus Luther lectured on Genesis where Joseph told his brothers, "You meant it for evil, but God meant it for good" (Genesis 50:20). So it goes with the church in this life. Quipped Luther, "We see only groaning, tears, troubles, and oppression of the poor; we see the devil's behind; we do not see the face of God." And yet just as God Himself worked all for good in the life of Joseph, St. Paul and in the cross of Jesus, so He works all for the good of the church and the Gospel. God is at work in it all, but this remains a matter of faith, not sight.

Things got convoluted very quickly (and intentionally) during and after my testimony before the House Committee on Government Oversight on February 16, 2012. I stepped into that "monkey cage" for one reason: The Health and Human Services provision requiring church-owned and related institutions to provide contraceptives (including drugs used intentionally to kill life in the womb) is a clear violation of the First Amendment rights of religious people. Moreover, even though our Concordia Health Plan is "grandfathered" in the policy—so that we are not forced to provide such drugs to our 50,000 participating church workers and their families—this very provision freezes our health plan in perpetuity. In essence, we are stuck between very narrow walls and no longer have the freedom to make the best economic choices for the benefit of our congregations and workers. This, too, is a violation of our religious freedoms.

The bologna came fast and furious. I refused to take the bait when Republicans tried to get me to carte blanche condemn the Obama administration. The Democrats created a sideshow, which worked. The media went on a feeding frenzy. The issue was soon framed in terms of "women's access to health care." My photo (along with the four other clergy on the panel) was shown far and wide and used by political opportunists with the most vile of rhetoric. The caption: "The Church does not care about women."

No argument in the hearing was truly heard. In fact, our antagonists weren't even in the room. They were busy running out and grabbing the next sheet of talking points to lob the next grenade.

Regrets? None. The issue is simple. We are not telling the government not to provide drugs or health care for women. We are not pushing for legislation to limit access to anything. Our own health plan *does* provide medications for specific health needs (which in other cases are used as contraceptives). I would argue that contraceptives (which the LCMS does not reject out of hand) and abortion-causing drugs are as available as bottled water in this culture of death. The "accommodation" offered by the president is a red herring. "Churches and their institutions won't pay for offensive medications; their insurers will." Oh? Most Catholic health plans are *self*-insured, just as the Concordia Health Plan is. At the end of the day, the issue is purely and simply about religious freedom.

The government is seeking to narrow and redefine religious freedom down to merely what churches do in houses of worship, and not a matter of their health, educational and other institutions. The US Constitution is on our side. But that isn't what gives me solace.

"Therefore let us learn not to follow our own thoughts or to measure and understand by our own counsels our misfortunes or works and experiences. . . . Before the world Christ is killed, condemned, and descends into hell. But before God this is the salvation of the whole world from the beginning all the way to the end" (Luther).

I was delighted to be ridiculed by the world. And I am especially delighted to know that precisely through cross, trial and ill-report, God works His good things. Count on it.

Concerning *Obergefell v. Hodges*

In a landmark 5–4 ruling on June 26, 2015, the US Supreme Court ruled that same-sex couples have a right to marry in any state in America, even in states where same-sex marriage currently is not recognized. President Harrison released the following letter that same day.

> God is our refuge and strength,
>   a very present help in trouble.
>
> Therefore we will not fear though the earth gives way,
>   though the mountains be moved into the heart
>   of the sea,
>
> though its waters roar and foam,
>   though the mountains tremble at its swelling. Selah
>
> There is a river whose streams make glad the city
>   of God,
>   the holy habitation of the Most High.
>
> God is in the midst of her; she shall not be moved;
>   God will help her when morning dawns.
>
> The nations rage, the kingdoms totter;
>   he utters his voice, the earth melts.
>
> The Lord of hosts is with us;
>   the God of Jacob is our fortress. (Psalm 46:1–7)

A one-person majority of the US Supreme Court got it wrong —again. Some 40 years ago, a similarly activist court legalized the killing of children in the womb. That decision has to date left a wake of some 58 million Americans dead. Today, the Court has imposed same-sex marriage upon the whole nation in a similar fashion. Five justices cannot determine natural or divine law. Now shall come the time of testing for Christians faithful to the Scriptures and the divine institution of marriage (Matthew 19:3–6), and indeed, a time of testing much more intense than what followed *Roe v. Wade*.

Like *Roe v. Wade*, this decision will be followed by a rash of lawsuits. Through coercive litigation, governments and popular culture continue to make the central postmodern value of sexual freedom override "the free exercise of religion" enshrined in the Bill of Rights.

The ramifications of this decision are seismic. Proponents will seek to drive Christians and Christian institutions out of education at all levels; they will press laws to force faithful Christian institutions and individuals to violate consciences in work practices and myriad other ways. We will have much more to say about this.

During some of the darkest days of Germany, a faithful Lutheran presciently described how governments lose their claim to legitimate authority according to Romans 13.

The Caesar cult in its manifold forms, the deification of the state, is one great form of the defection from the [true] idea of the state. There are also other possibilities of such defection. The government can forget and neglect its tasks. When it no longer distinguishes between right and wrong, when its courts are no longer governed by the strict desire for justice, but by special interests, when government no longer has the courage to exercise its law, fails to exercise its duties, undermines its own legal order, when it weakens through its family law parental authority and the estate of marriage, then it ceases to be governing authority.

Raising such a question can lead to heavy conflicts of conscience. But it is fundamentally conceivable, and it has time and again become reality in history, that a governing authority has ceased to be governing authority. In such a case there may indeed exist a submission to a superior power. But the duty of obedience against this power no longer exists. (Hermann Sasse, "What Is the State?" [1932])

As faithful Christians, we shall continue to be obedient to just laws. We affirm the human rights of all individuals and the inherent and equal value of all people. We respect the divinely given dignity of all people, no matter their sexual preference. We recognize that, under the exacting and demanding laws of God, we are indeed sinners in thought, word and deed, just as are all (Romans 3:9ff.). We confess that the "blood of Jesus Christ, God's Son, cleanses us from all our sins" (1 John 1:7). We confess that God's divine law of marriage and the entire Ten Commandments apply to all, and that so also the life-giving sacrifice of Christ on the cross is for all. It is a "righteousness of God through faith in Jesus Christ for all who believe" (Romans 3:22).

However, even as we struggle as a church to come to a unified response to this blatant rejection of the entire history of human-kind and its practice of marriage, "we shall obey God rather than man" (Acts 5:29). Christians will now begin to learn what it means to be in a state of solemn conscientious objection against the state. We will resist its imposition of falsehood upon us, even as we continue to reach out to those who continue to be harmed by the ethic of radical sexual freedom, detached from God's blessing of marriage. And we will stand shoulder to shoulder with Christians, churches, and people of goodwill who are resolute on this issue.

God help us. Amen.

God's Gift of Life

The lie is the death of man, his temporal and his eternal death. The lie kills nations. The most powerful nations of the world have been laid waste because of their lies. History knows of no more unsettling sight than the judgment rendered upon the people of an advanced culture who have rejected the truth and are swallowed upon in a sea of lies. Where this happens, as in the case of declining pagan antiquity, religion and law, poetry and philosophy, life in marriage and family, in the state and society—in short, one sphere of life after another falls sacrifice to the power and curse of the lie. Where man can no longer bear the truth, he cannot live without the lie. Where man denies that he and others are dying, the terrible dissolution [of his culture] is held up as a glorious ascent, and decline is viewed as an advance, the likes of which has never been experienced.

(Hermann Sasse, "Union and Confession" in *The Lonely Way,* vol. 1 [Concordia Publishing House, 2001], p. 266.)

L ike few other conservative Lutherans in Germany in 1933, Hermann Sasse recognized in Nazism the mystery of evil mentioned by St. Paul. "For we do not wrestle against flesh and blood, but against the rulers, against the authorities, against the cosmic powers over this present darkness, against the spiritual forces of evil in the heavenly places" (Ephesians 6:12). The world largely ignored the murder of six million human beings by the Nazis, whom the latter regarded as a "decadent" race, ignored at least until the prison camps were opened, and photos and films were released to a world aghast. Sadly, the aged Luther's vitriolic attacks on the Jews for not accepting the Gospel (not on racial grounds, as in the case of the Nazis) only added anti-Semitic fuel to the horrid fire.

Forty years after *Roe v. Wade,* we—the soldiers and very liberators of Germany from the darkness of the Third Reich—have largely ignored and continue to ignore the deaths of some 50,000,000 innocent unborn babies in "the land of the free," where we are allegedly guaranteed "life, liberty and the pursuit of happiness."

After a Shooting in South Carolina

Another brutal and senseless killing spree by a crazed gunman, motivated by racial hatred, sends our thoughts swirling between despair and numbness. Why were these nine Christians martyred as they were taking in the life-giving Word of God in Christian Bible study? We know and are too often reminded that there is horrid evil in this world, and an "evil one" who bedevils the minds of such killers. Jesus said it would be so (John 17:15).

As the world devolves around us from insanity to insanity, I'm reminded of this statement from John Adams: "Our Constitution was made only for a moral and religious people. It is wholly inadequate to the government of any other." Nowhere is that more true than in the case of the Second Amendment. As both religion and morality are on steep decline among us, we can expect only more of this insanity by individuals unhinged from the safety of families and a society normed by natural law and influenced by the genuine teaching of the Bible. "Love your neighbor as yourself" (Mark 12:31).

No truth of the New Testament is so loudly stated by Jesus than that the Triune God is the Creator of all people (Matthew 19:4); that God loves all (John 3:16); that all are equally indebted to God and valuable to him (2 Corinthians 5:14–15; John 8:12). Racism is a fundamental denial of the Word of God (cf. Acts 2:5ff.; Matthew 15:21ff.) and natural law. "We hold these truths to be self-evident, that all men are created equal" (Declaration of Independence). The denial of human rights, maltreatment of persons due to race, including the forbidding of the right for a man and a woman to marry without regard to race, is contrary to natural and divinely revealed law (Holy Scripture). It also contradicts the universality of the truth of the Gospel of Christ, who died for all (Romans 3:9–10, 19; 2 Corinthians 5:19).

We mourn the loss of these dear Christians and pray for their loved ones. May they be consoled by "the resurrection of the body and the life everlasting" and the picture of heaven painted by St. John in Revelation of "a great multitude that no one could number, from every nation, from all tribes and peoples and languages, standing before the throne and before the Lamb, clothed in white robes, with palm branches in their hands" (7:9).

114

We reject racism and racially motivated hatred in all its forms. We repent where we have fallen short, and we pray for strength to stand for what is good and right and true. We pray for the perpetrator and his family, even as we demand the swift execution of justice.

Lord, have mercy upon us.

A Letter to Pastors during Election Year 2016

Dear Brothers in the Office of the Ministry,

> I thank my God in all my remembrance of you, always in every prayer of mine for you all making my prayer with joy, because of your partnership in the gospel from the first day until now. And I am sure of this, that he who began a good work in you will bring it to completion at the day of *Jesus Christ.* (Philippians 1:3–6)

I dare say we would all agree that this is the most interesting if not strangest election cycle we've ever seen. I thought I'd spill a bit of ink on the topic of the two kingdoms doctrine and a Lutheran approach to politics. I know full well from experience how delicate, and even explosive, these issues can be for a pastor as an election year intensifies.

It's a fact that the overwhelming majority of LCMS clergy are Republicans. (Not too long ago, a poll of LCMS pastors in the state of Wisconsin found that 95 percent of our clergy there self-describe as either "conservative Republican" or "very conservative Republican.") The laity also lean toward the right, but with much less intensity than the clergy. Add to this the fact that the few issues that the LCMS has taken a public stance on also are preferred issues of the political right (life, marriage, and religious freedom), and this makes for a potentially precarious, if not volatile, mix for pastors, preaching, and congregations!

Last year, I wrote in *The Lutheran Witness* about a very interesting connection between James Madison and the Lutheran two kingdoms doctrine.

> Late in 1821, Rev. Frederick Schaeffer presided over the cornerstone laying of a new building for the Evangelical Lutheran Church of St. Matthew in New York City. Afterward, he sent his homily to James Madison, the "Father of the US Constitution" and chief author of the Bill of Rights.

Pastor Schaeffer's address was rather strongly Lutheran, in spite of the general weakness of
American Lutheranism prior to 1840.

Madison replied:

Montpellier, Dec. 3rd, 1821

Revd Sir,—I have received, with your letter of
November 19th, the copy of your address at the cer-
emonial of laying the corner-stone of St Matthew's
Church in New York.

It is a pleasing and persuasive example of pious
zeal, united with pure benevolence and of a cordial
attachment to a particular creed, untinctured with
sectarian illiberality. It illustrates the excellence of
a system which, by a due distinction, to which the
genius and courage of Luther led the way, between
what is due to Caesar and what is due God, best promotes the discharge of both obligations. The experience of the United States is a happy disproof of the
error so long rooted in the unenlightened minds of
well-meaning Christians, as well as in the corrupt
hearts of persecuting usurpers, that without a legal
incorporation of religious and civil polity, neither
could be supported. A mutual independence is found
most friendly to practical Religion, to social harmony,
and to political prosperity.

In return for your kind sentiments, I tender assurances of my esteem and my best wishes.

James Madison

Don't you find it interesting that one of the chief architects
of the US Constitution and the Bill of Rights says, "Luther led the
way"? I do.

Madison states, "What is due to Caesar and what is due God,
best promotes the discharge of both obligations." Luther wrote,
"Church leaders make poor kings and kings make poor bishops"
(Luther's Works 45:109). Luther recognized, on the basis of Jesus'
words in the New Testament, "Render to Caesar the things that are
Caesar's, and to God the things that are God's" (Mark 12:17), that

there are two distinct realms. The state is ruled by reason, and the church is ruled by the Word of God. Both are indeed God's, but He governs them differently. The one is the realm of Law and reason; the other is the Word of God and Gospel. "For rulers are not a terror to good conduct, but to bad . . . for he is God's servant for your good. But if you do wrong, be afraid, for he does not bear the sword in vain" (Romans 13:3–4).

Luther, in the wake of more than a millennium of confusion of church and state, got the New Testament right. Whatever inconsistencies in practice, Luther recognized that passages such as "If you abide in my word, you are truly my disciples, and you will know the truth, and the truth will set you free" (John 8:31–32) meant that the religious mind of mankind is not subject to the coercion of temporal authority.

In his book *Tyranny and Resistance: The Magdeburg Confession and the Lutheran Tradition* (CPH, 2001), David Mark Whitford notes three approaches to the questions of "what is due God" and "what is due to Caesar." These were all current at the time of the Reformation and have obvious influence yet today.

1. The *inclusively ecclesial* view: "Authority for the governance of creation is founded by God in the church. God's authority flows to the church (and especially the pope); the church then yields some of that authority to the emperor. As far back as Pope Leo's bold move to crown Charlemagne emperor of the Romans (AD 800), Leo began the establishment of papal supremacy over secular authority" (Whitford, p. 31).

2. The *exclusively biblical* model: "The church must conform to the Gospel explicitly [i.e., including theocratic ideas from the Old Testament]. No deviation is allowed. The relationship between the secular and spiritual is antagonistic. This antagonism seems to elicit two responses: withdrawal [e.g., the Amish] or usurpation [i.e., the state must conform to the Bible, traditional Calvinism]. In many Anabaptist groups, the church withdrew from secular society and placed itself over and against the dominant culture. In some respects, this model is a resurrection and modification of the ecclesial model. The church must conform to the whole Bible, and the state as well. Both Andreas Bodenstein von Karlstadt and Thomas Muentzer fall into this category" (Whitford, p. 31).

3. Again, from Whitford: The third approach differs significantly from both the inclusively ecclesial and exclusively biblical models. Often labeled *magisterial, the inclusively biblical approach* is epitomized by Luther's doctrine of the two realms. In Luther's thought, each realm is part of God's plan for ordering creation. The spiritual realm is eternal and everlasting; it is the realm of revelation and faith. Instantiated in the church, it exists to offer the grace of God to all through preaching the Word of God and celebrating the sacraments. . . . Like the Law to Gospel, the secular realm is the spiritual realm's dialectical partner; it is the realm of reason and unbelief. Both the secular and spiritual exist for God's regulation of creation, but like Law and Gospel, they play different roles. Whereas the spiritual realm is eternal and proleptic, the secular is finite and fleeting. Here the sword instead of service is definitive" (Whitford, pp. 31–32).

Model 1 has been very significantly moderated by Vatican II, and today we find Roman Catholics very helpful in struggles for life, marriage, and religious freedom. Model 2 is one that often affects or pulls in Lutherans who argue for America as a "Christian nation." America certainly has been that. America was certainly dominated by Christian founders (despite the Deism and religious liberalism of men like Jefferson, who as President, by the way, went to church every Sunday . . . in the House Chambers!). We can only say "America was founded on the Bible" with a strong caveat. If by that we mean that the Bible *as revelation* is the authority for government, then this is false. When the Declaration of Independence states, "We hold these truths to be self-evident, that all men are created equal, that they are endowed by their Creator with certain unalienable rights," this is arrived at through reason, not revelation. In other words, it is important to realize that the founders did not believe it reasonable to believe that there was no Creator! They were right. "The fool says in his heart, 'There is no God'" (Psalm 14:1). It is more precise and correct for us to state that this nation was founded upon reason, and reason, when it is working—that is, when it is most reasonable—accords with the ethical teaching of the Ten Commandments (Romans 1:14–15). The ethical teaching of the Ten Commandments, and thus Christianity, profoundly marked the founding of the United States. Nevertheless, the church and state were kept distinct. The state may coerce, punish, wage war, etc., but only so far as God-given inalienable rights are recognized and guarded. The state may not coerce the religious conscience; that conscience is responsible to God. To paraphrase a quote of Luther, "The state and the religious conscience are not good bedfellows. The bed is too narrow and the blanket too short!" Our founders recognized what so many courts and political leaders today have forgotten. A government favorable to responsible religion, particularly Christianity, causes a nation to thrive.

I would urge that all of us carefully work through the Apology of the Augsburg Confession XVI on political power with our Bible classes and congregations. It says, "Christ's kingdom is spiritual." "The Gospel does not introduce laws about the public state, but is the forgiveness of sins and the beginning of a new life in the hearts of believers. The Gospel not only approves outward governments, but also subjects us to them (Romans 13:1)." *This is vital for us to remember, particularly when we object to laws that have allowed 58 million abortions, same-sex marriage, and an ever increasing encroachment upon religious freedom.* These matters, as vital as they are, are ultimately important only as they intersect and impact *the chief purpose of the church*, which Jesus put so clearly and simply: "The Son of Man came to seek and to save the lost" (Luke 19:10).

As Christian pastors, what can we preach during this volatile year? Should we openly support a particular party or candidate in our preaching? Of course not! Should we say, "If you vote for this or that person, you can't be a Christian"? Certainly not! Our people have individual experiences in life that guide the exercise of their vote as citizens. For one, it might be hassling with the IRS in a small business. For another, it might be trying to work for better treatment and benefits for factory workers. Another may have grown up in the South under Jim Crow laws. Our people will make their political decisions on the basis of any number of factors that may, at times, mystify us. At times such as these, it is also appropriate, dear pastors (no matter where your particular political propensities lie), to recall that wonderful teaching of Franz Pieper: the "felicitous inconsistency."

What can we preach? We can urge our people to be politically active and to stand in the public square for what accords with reason and the Ten Commandments. We can preach that we as Christian citizens will join with all people of goodwill to promote and care for life, from womb to grave; we will support traditional marriage; and we shall oppose laws, courts, and governments restricting *our God-*

given rights—rights that were acknowledged by the Bill of Rights as inherent (not granted!). We shall urge our people to be knowledgeable about candidates' positions on issues that the Bible speaks about and on which the church has taken a stand, and to take these issues into consideration as they make their choices.

We must be quite careful not to coerce political activity. Coercion is not the business of the church [FC SD X 15]. We must avoid in every way the impression that politics or controverted issues are front and center and the Gospel is set in the background (1 Corinthians 1:23; 2:2). We must take care not to allow our politics (which may take positions on all sorts of issues about which the Word of God and the church are silent) to skew our theology and preaching! I may have a political view that there should be a wall on the border. But that doesn't change one iota of Christ's mandate to care for the illegal/undocumented neighbor who might well be living or working next to me. (Consider Jesus' love for the "unclean" Samaritans and even pagans; John 4; Matthew 15:21; Luke 10:25–37; Hebrews 13:1). I might have strong views on Muslim immigration, but that dare not make me unwilling and unable to see that these people are in my community already, and they need Christ (Matthew 9:37; John 3:16; Revelation 7:9; 1 Corinthians 2:2). When the requirements of the two realms clash in this sinful world, the Gospel must predominate. "We must obey God rather than men" (Acts 5:29).

Above all, brothers, preach and teach Christ. By the blessed power of the Gospel, He continues to work the miracles of forgiveness, life, and salvation. Both Madison's comments and the Lutheran doctrine of the two kingdoms beg for more discussion, but alas, that shall have to wait for another occasion.

As we continue together on the road of repentance toward Good Friday (and the parallel path of pain, antics, joys, and disappointments during the political season), God grant you the strength of mind, body, and soul to serve Him in word and deed. And I join all of you in fervent prayer for our nation and its leaders, present and future.

"Now may the God of peace who brought again from the dead our Lord Jesus, the great shepherd of the sheep, by the blood of the eternal covenant, equip you with everything good that you may do his will, working in us that which is pleasing in his sight, through Jesus Christ, to whom be glory forever and ever. Amen" (Hebrews 13:20–21).

Thanks for all you do, dear brothers.

Family and Vocation

The Joy of Family

I was just a boy. Our life was simple, our house small, our family inauspicious. But Mom and Dad never failed to find ways to add a little fun to life. One Christmas, Dad brought home a snowmobile to two boys, gazing, mouths agape out the front window. It was only minutes later that my brother and I were dressed for the weather and climbing about this sleek machine, itching for the first shot at it. It was a brilliant move for the family. Every weekend or holiday when snow prevailed in northwest Iowa, we'd haul the machine out to Cousin Larry's farm and spend the afternoon together. Dad would pull us via rope on an old truck tire inner tube over snow-covered hill and dale. We'd try to hang on, only to lose the battle higgledy-piggledy in a tumble of arms, legs, snow and laughter. I can see in my mind's eye my dad on that machine, one knee kneeling on the seat (as he liked to ride), head held high above the windshield, grinning ear to ear, glasses fogged, circling to give us another go at it. "Do it again, Dad! Again!"

My little sister, who to this day retains something of her unique combination of timidity and total self-confidence, had decided it was time for her to solo on the snow machine. Dad cautiously consented, offered the requisite instruction and warnings. He pointed her in a safe direction. My brother and I braced for the boredom, reduced to making snow angels. Little Sis took her first spin at the speed of a glacier, tediously consuming our treasured minutes of icy, rough-and-tumble racing and daring.

As she pulled away, Dad watched her traverse every snow-covered inch. I noticed him growing anxious as Sister increased to moderate speed and headed in the direction of a barbed wire fence at the edge of the property. Concerned for her safety, he cupped his hands and began to shout her name, warning her away from the fence, already leaning and stepping toward her. Then (and I shall never forget it because it is the only time I'd ever seen my father run flat out) fearing for her safety, he took off at full speed, shouting her name. Of all my childhood memories, this one stands forever uniquely etched upon the palette of my mind. I saw my father in dark green coveralls, gloves and snow boots, running as fast as he could over an uneven fallow field, through a foot of snow, anxiously screaming my sister's name. I was face-to-face with the depth of love of a father for his child.

I know to this day that this man, so very understated and in many ways so unanimated, is animated by an incomprehensively deep love for my mom, my sister, my brother and me—and for Jesus. And it has always given me profound joy to realize it and recall it. As if his running angst were itself a prayer, my sister— completely oblivious to her father's snow-muffled shouts—was gently carried out of danger. . . .

"He giveth power to the faint; and to them that have no might he increaseth strength. Even the youths shall faint and be weary, and the young men shall utterly fall: But they that wait upon the Lord shall renew their strength; they shall mount up with wings as eagles; they shall run, and not be weary" (Isaiah 40:29–31). . . .

There are many accounts in the Bible of saints running at the joy of seeing Jesus. Zacchaeus "ran ahead and climbed a sycamore tree to see him" (Luke 19:3). "Peter rose and ran to the tomb" (Luke 24:12). The women "departed quickly from the tomb with fear and great joy, and ran to tell his disciples" (Matthew 28:8). There are also accounts of false saints running with pseudo joy. The demoniac, "when he saw Jesus from afar, ran and fell down before him" (Mark 5:6). Even the rich young man ran to Jesus to pose his horrid, Gospel-denying question: "A man ran up and knelt before him and asked him, 'Good Teacher, what must I do to inherit eternal life?'" (Mark 10:17).

But Jesus' parable of the prodigal son provides the grandest sprint ever recorded. It unveils for us the heart of God the Father in Christ. Our God rejoices over sinners and sprints to show it.

—(Excerpted from *A Little Book on Joy* [CPH, 2011], pp. 66–70.)

Marriage and the Church

Someone quipped, "The world is moving *so fast* these days that the one who says it can't be done is generally interrupted by someone doing it." I thought rather cynically about this quote as I listened to the Supreme Court argue over the Defense of Marriage Act (DOMA). Just a decade and a half ago, this legislation was signed into law, defining marriage for federal purposes as the union of one man and one woman. DOMA came as a safeguard against individual states redefining marriage and forcing the federal government (the whole nation!) to treat same-sex "marriage" as legitimate.

Two sources tell us what marriage is. First, the Bible tells us that man and woman were created by God as the perfect match, and that marriage is to be a sacred, lifelong union of one man and one woman. The Bible universally rejects sex outside of this man/woman marriage. Second, we know from so-called natural knowledge, which is part of all human existence, and which has been codified by custom and law through the millennia, that marriage is for one man and one woman. It is God's perfectly designed institution for the creation of new human life and for the nurture of civilized individuals. As Luther famously noted in his Large Catechism, "If he won't obey his parents, he'll obey the hangman!"

What has come with lightning speed is merely the summation of a long process of the devaluation of marriage in Western culture. In 1970, only one state had no-fault divorce. By 1980, 49 had it. Coterminously, marriage has increasingly come to be defined as an emotional bond with a significant other rather than a fundamental building block of all society, religion and culture, based upon the fact that a man and a woman choose to enter a solemn lifelong contract and bring new life into this world.

The Supreme Court will likely rule on the two cases (DOMA and Proposition 8) in late June. Like *Roe v. Wade*, which found a (fictional) right to abortion in the US Constitution, the court could rule that the traditional definition of marriage of one man and one woman is unconstitutional. No matter how the court rules, the fight has just begun. Many in our own fellowship think, "What's the big deal? Isn't it just about widening the tent of tolerance a bit more?" If that were it, it would be a major relief. But it's not. What's at stake is our First Amendment right to the free exercise of our religious conviction in the way we act in society. As the same-sex marriage train gains steam, we find ourselves increasingly under attack, and our social ministry agencies are forced to either capitulate to the state or lose funding and even licenses. All opposed to same-sex marriage for conscience grounds are and will increasingly be labeled "bigots" in line with slave-holders and those who were opposed to ending legalized racism in this country. And know this: As traditional Christians are driven out of the public square, the door is also closed for the Gospel.

The task before us is monumental. We are called to repent of our lack of appreciation for marriage and family. We are called to confess Christ to all and call all to repentance. We must elevate marriage among us and educate, educate, educate. Even as we seek specific ways to care for those challenged by same-sex attraction, we must resist conforming to the culture.

We know whose we are. We know what is in store for us. We know we will be severely tested in these last days, but this testing will abound in faithfulness and praise (1 Peter 1).

Why Should the Average Lutheran Kid Go to Church?

(A Letter to My Two Teenage Boys)

Okay, guys. I've never told you that "you are the future of the Church." And I never will. The Bible says the Church is "built on the foundation of the apostles and prophets, Jesus Christ himself being the chief cornerstone" (Ephesians 2:20). Jesus is the future of the Church. Jesus is "the same yesterday, today and forever" (Hebrews 13:8). Jesus has a future, and so every person connected to Jesus has a future.

That's why, more than anything else, your mom and I want you connected with Jesus. That's why I baptized each of you. That's why we read all the Bible stories to you as toddlers. That's why we have a time of devotion when we can actually eat together. That's why we've prayed for you from day one. That's why we sent you to a Lutheran grade school. That's why we made sure you knew the catechism. That's why we always go to church. And that's why we are LCMS Lutherans. The LCMS is simply the best thing going because for orthodox Lutherans, it's all about Jesus— all about being connected to Jesus.

The Church has a profound responsibility to pay attention to young people. The Bible teaches that all over the place. Today, the Missouri Synod has just less than half the high-school-age young people that it had when I graduated from Sioux City, East High in 1980. Why? Mainly because we've just followed the national trend of European-descent Americans who are having fewer children.

In any case, as LCMS young people, you are a precious commodity, indeed! But don't let that go to your heads. The Bible teaches that young people are very much prone to particular and serious sins. "Remember not the sins of my youth" (Psalm 25:7). And I hardly have to tell you what they are. Luther said the sins of youth tend to be sexual, while the sins of old age are greed. All sin condemns. "The wages of sin is death" (Romans 6:23). I've never pulled any punches in teaching you what the Bible says about sin. We deserve hell, pure and simple. "But the free gift of God is eternal life in Christ Jesus" (Romans 6:23). And so we've always spoken forgiveness at home to each other. We're sinners.

We are forgiven sinners. And so we sinners forgive others who sin against us. We are Gospel people to those around us. Christianity is not about ethics. It's about Jesus.

The Sunday liturgy shows you why we go to church. Luther said we are beggars who stand before God with an empty sack. What happens in the liturgy? The pastor starts us off in the Name of the Triune God. God's there to do His stuff! Then in the confession of sins, "I, a poor miserable sinner . . ." we say, "Dear God, I've got an empty sack!" If you don't think you're a sinner, if you don't think your bag's empty, you'll never understand why we go to church. "In the stead and by the command of my Lord Jesus Christ I forgive you all your sins," says the pastor. He drops a load of forgiveness, grace and mercy into your bag. And you say, "Amen! Yup! It's in my bag!" Then the Scriptures are read, and more grace and Gospel and mercy are dropped in. Then the sermon is preached, and you are told that you are damned by the Law, but that Jesus comes *only for sinners.* Hooray! "I came not for the righteous but the unrighteous" (Mark 2:17). And at the end of the sermon, you say (and don't leave this to the pastor), "Amen! Got 'er in the bag!" Then you kneel at the altar to receive the body and blood of Jesus. "Take and eat, Christ's body and blood for you, for the forgiveness of all your sins." And you say again, "Amen! It's in my bag!" This continues right through the Aaronic blessing: "The Lord bless you and keep you, make His face shine upon you, and give you peace."

"Amen! Amen! Amen! It's in the bag. I've got it tied up and hoisted on my shoulder as I head out of church."

Now, how shall I live with that big bag of forgiveness, grace and mercy? When my dad sins against me, what do I do? I open my bag and say, "Here, Dad. You misunderstood me and thought ill of me, but I forgive you 'cause I've been forgiven." Then that teacher at school drives you crazy, and you open your bag again. Then that awful bully harasses and embarrasses you, and when your emotions calm, you open your bag of grace and pray, "Forgive him, Lord. He doesn't know what he's doing. And he's hurting inside big time." Then you run into a friend who's really in need because her home life is chaos, and you show her love and compassion like Jesus. In fact, the mercy of Jesus is the greatest compelling factor for you to live a meaningful life of service and love to others.

This happens all week long. Then comes Sunday morning, and you find yourself in church again confessing, "Dear God, I've got an empty sack."

Honestly, boys, I'm frightened for you. This world is an absolute mess. But I'm also confident. Jesus grabbed you at the font, and He won't let go. "No one can snatch them out of my hand" (John 10:28). I'm proud of how you've grown. I'm proud of how you've stood the test. I'm proud of how you've kindly witnessed to Jesus in your young lives. And I'm absolutely sure the Church has a future because Jesus has a future, and He's made you His very own for eternity. "Be thou faithful unto death and I will give you the crown of life" (Revelation 2:10).

Dad

Taboo: The Things We're Not Talking About

To my brothers and sisters in college:

Nobody knows what's *taboo* in this world better than you. Each day in school and at work, you're bombarded with what's acceptable to speak about and what's not, what's okay to bring up in front of your professors and friends and what you can't, which words and phrases and ideas are acceptable to hold and which aren't.

And that means that you know just how taboo the Christian understanding is of sex, marriage and gender. Dare to tell someone you are waiting to have sex until you're married, and you'll get the hairy eyeball. Explain that you believe marriage is between one man and one woman, and you'll be labeled "bigoted" and "intolerant."

It's enough to make a Lutheran college student want to clam up and run. But our Lord teaches you to do the exact opposite, and that's why He's put parents and pastors in your life to help you articulate what Jesus has to say about difficult matters; they can share how to speak the truth in love and why it's not so scary to confess Christ in the public square after all.

Defending the faith, especially in university classrooms and college quads, will be one of the most difficult things you'll do. Yet, from Holy Scripture, you'll be reminded of the power of God's Word. You'll be reminded of the gifts given to you in your Baptism that enable you to confess what you know to be true on account of Christ. You'll be reminded of Jesus, who sees nothing and no one as taboo, but who loves to forgive and comfort His children.

You are baptized into Christ, and that means that your beliefs and confession will be taboo to the world. But . . . you are baptized into Christ, and that means that no college professor or campus group can snatch you from Him, from the One who loves you, who died for you and who rose again . . . all for you!

By the love of God the Father, who chose a young woman to carry out His plan of salvation, a young woman who knew what it is to be confused by an unplanned pregnancy; by the grace of Christ, who while still in the womb was greeted by the "leaping," yes, "rejoicing" John the Baptizer, himself unborn (Luke 1:44); by the strength of Him who healed every disease and cared for every life He encountered (Mark 1:34); by the mercy of God the Father who sent His Son, mercy incarnate for all (Luke 1:78); by the knowledge of our eternal God and Lord who knows and loves every child formed in the womb (Jeremiah 1:5; John 3:16); empowered by the Spirit of life who gives me life (Job 33:4; Romans 8:10), I—a sinner no better than the next (1 Timothy 1:15)—shall speak (Jeremiah 20:9). I shall intervene (Luke 10:33). I shall love all and treasure God's gift of life, womb to tomb (1 Timothy 6:18). For Jesus experienced it all, sanctified it all and redeems it all (Galatians 3:13). He has redeemed me that I may no longer live for myself (1 John 4:9; 1 Peter 4:2).

"Men, why are you doing these things? We also are men, of like nature with you, and we bring you good news, that you should turn from these vain things to a living God, who made the heaven and the earth and the sea and all that is in them" (Acts 14:15).

For the sake of LIFE.

The Joy of Everyday Life

The word for "church" in the New Testament is *ecclesia*. It means, literally, "called out." Christians are "called out" by Christ—out of and away from sin, death, and the devil. But this does not mean that we are called away from living real lives, or as Luther put it, should "live in a corner." To be sure, Jesus from time to time retreated to "rest for a while" (Mark 6:31) with his apostles, but quickly returned to the fray, to his sacred vocation of accomplishing our salvation. Our souls find their "rest" in Christ (Matthew 11:29), but this very spiritual peace and joy in Christ drives us back into life with both feet. If peace is joy at rest, then happily meddling in the affairs of folks around us who need us is joy in action.

The secret to living a good news life in a bad news world is coming to the deep conviction that the high callings of God, the vocations that he regards as great and marvelous, are those in which we serve folks right under our nose. "There is [according to Martin Luther] nothing more delightful and lovable on earth than one's neighbor. Love does not think about works, it finds joy in people" (Gustaf Wingren, *Luther on Vocation* [Muhlenberg, 1957], 43). The gravitational pull of Christ draws us to Himself for grace and mercy and peace and joy, and then hurls us into the world around us. For the great majority of us, that does not mean being called to serve as a missionary in Africa, or even as a pastor or deaconess or parochial school teacher. It means that we are driven—freely compelled ("The love of Christ compels us"; 2 Corinthians 5:14)—to serve our spouse in love, to care for our children, to help our next-door neighbor, to help the poor, hurting and suffering in our church, to love our grandparents, and to serve our community. And no matter what or where our calling, we are placed in a context to serve those right around us. "Truly, I say to you, as you did it to one of the least of these my brothers, you did it to me" (Matthew 25:40). That goes as much for changing diapers as it does for slogging to make a buck to put food on the table and pay the bills. "For whatever does not proceed from faith is sin" (Romans 14:23). But it is also true that whatever we do in faith is delightful and pleasing to God. We can do it with full confidence that, in Christ, all our sins are covered, and our vocations as father, mother, son, daughter, clerk, farmer, technician, teacher, fireman, or nurse are vocations in which the Lord delights with joy.

But God chose what is foolish in the world to shame the wise; God chose what is weak in the world to shame the strong; God chose what is low and despised in the world, even things that are not, to bring to nothing things that are, so that no human being might boast in the presence of God. And because of him you are in Christ Jesus, who became to us wisdom from God, righteousness and sanctification and redemption, so that, as it is written, "Let the one who boasts, boast in the Lord." (1 Corinthians 1:27–31)

—(Excerpted from *A Little Book on Joy* [CPH, 2011], pp. 153–59.)

Joy Over Life

Joy over life verily leaps off the pages of Holy Writ. It bubbles from the mouth of Jesus. It animates His every action. There is—in addition to specific, pervasive and persuasive texts (Genesis 1:26, 27; 9:6; Exodus 21:22–25)—an ethic of the inherent value of every human life conceived, no matter its form or malformity. Simply put, for Jesus there is no "life unworthy of life." In fact, Christ turns the human value system completely on its head (1 Corinthians 1:25, 27) to the great delight and joy of the "least."

And when Elizabeth heard the greeting of Mary, the baby leaped [literally "skipped"] in her womb. And Elizabeth was filled with the Holy Spirit, and she exclaimed with a loud cry, "Blessed are you among women, and blessed is the fruit of your womb! And why is this granted to me that the mother of my Lord should come to me? For behold, when the sound of your greeting came to my ears, the baby in my womb leaped for joy" (Luke 1:41–44).

What a remarkable transaction! John the Baptizer "skips for joy" *in utero* over the greeting of "the mother of my Lord." Two unborns (the Lord Himself and His great forerunner) are each acknowledged as such in the womb! The word (used by Luke more than any other New Testament writer) expresses what is an "outburst of joy." Luke is indeed the "evangelist of joy" and more. He's the "evangelist of the joy over life!"

A peasant, Elizabeth, rejoiced over the unborn Lord (Luke 1:42). The unlikely mother of the Lord, Mary, sang her Magnificat: "My spirit rejoices in God my Savior. . . . He has exalted those of humble estate" (Luke 1:46ff.). Elizabeth's friends and family rejoiced with her over her newborn (Luke 1:58). Zechariah's tongue was loosed in praise after the mute wrote, "His name is John. . . . He spoke, blessing God . . . for he has visited and redeemed his people" (Luke 1:63). Praise and blessing are the sounds that joy makes!

At the birth of Christ, the angel announced to the shepherds: "Fear not, for behold, I bring you good news of a great joy that will be for all the people" (Luke 2:10). The whole heavenly host rejoiced over the One who came to bring peace between God and man (Luke 2:14). Feeble, old Simeon beheld this very life—in his own arms, in the flesh and rejoiced! "Mine eyes have seen your salvation. . . . Let your servant depart in peace" (Luke 2:29). Peace is joy at rest.

There is much, much more in Luke's Gospel alone, including all the rejoicing over the prodigal, the lost coin, the great banquet . . . and finally, the greatest affirmation of human life in time for eternity, the resurrection of Jesus. After the Lord's ascension, "They worshiped him and returned to Jerusalem with great joy, and were continually in the temple blessing God" (Luke 24:52–53). Acts continues the exuberant theme of joy over life (Acts 2:26, 46; 5:41; 8:8, 39; 11:23; 12:14; 13:52). "In all things I [Paul] have shown you that by working hard in this way we must help the weak and remember the words of the Lord Jesus, how he himself said, 'It is more blessed to give than to receive'" (Acts 20:35). Each and every one of these references is a testament etched in stone bearing witness: there is no "life unworthy of living!"

—(Excerpted from *A Little Book on Joy* [CPH, 2011], pp. 91–95.)

Equal Value in God's Sight

In the church, we often say, "He's a called pastor," or "She's a called teacher, DCE, deaconess, etc." These calls to church workers happen by a definite and ordered process by an action of the congregation. God calls workers "mediately" or through means (Acts 14:23; 1 Timothy 4:14).

The Lutheran Reformation, however, is responsible for a more radical rediscovery. Everyone has vocations. Being "called to faith" by God in Christ brings a sanctification and value to all of life's relationships. Our vocations are determined by where we are put in this life. We have what Luther called "stations" in life, which exist in three main realms: the church; marriage, which includes all economic relationships; and the state.

As a Christian, I'm called to be president of the LCMS, and I'm a called assistant pastor at Village Lutheran, Ladue, Missouri. I'm also "called" in a different but certainly no less significant way to be a son, a husband, a brother, a dad, a friend, a neighbor. And finally, I have a vocation as a citizen. I am to honor the government (Romans 13:1ff.), be a good citizen in my community and be a good neighbor. And the Scriptures say much about all of these relationships!

The Lutheran Reformation reestablished the clear teaching of the equal value in God's sight of every station and vocation. The simplest or most humble station in life has the same duty as the most powerful and profound: to serve God and man. And to serve my neighbor (all those placed around me in my life) is to serve God. The most mundane callings and vocations in this life are holy and precious in God's sight. We are saved by the merit of Christ alone, not by our works. Because this is so, there simply are no good works or even vocations (so far as they are not sinful by definition) that are inherently less holy or more holy and pleasing to God. To be sure, some receive more honor, but it is a profound New Testament truth that the body "has many members" and "if one member is honored, all rejoice together" (1 Corinthians 12:12, 26).

As pastors, we have many important tasks. Like all vocations, the pastor's vocation is one of Christ-like service (Mark 10:45). One area of service is assisting lay people to realize their callings in the life of the church, the family and the state. Without the service and wisdom of laity, the LCMS ceases not only to function, but also to exist. There are specific duties that the Scriptures give to the Office of the Ministry. The people of a congregation call a man to carry out those duties (preach, teach, administer the Sacraments). A pastor renders holy service when he encourages lay people to take up vocations of service in the church and when he values the vocations of the laity and teaches them how remarkably significant and God-pleasing even the simplest (and least honored by the world) vocation is!

As I was getting ready to head to my first congregation, I informed old Dr. Degner at the Fort Wayne seminary that I was going to a small, rural community. I also made a disparaging remark about it. I'll never forget his wise rebuke: "Matt, you are going to find that those people will be the most industrious, smart and capable people you will ever know." Wow, was he right! What a pleasure it was to be trained to be a pastor by that first congregation. I beheld the beehive of activity of those farming and rural folks as they served their families, church and community in myriad ways, and most significantly, they shared Christ within their vocations to those around them. What an honor to serve there! They knew what they were doing, even when I didn't.

Understanding vocation is critical for the relationship of pastor and people. The early Missouri Lutherans were criticized heavily for allowing too much authority to the laity and balancing lay/clergy representation in the governance of the church. The second president of the Synod, Friedrich Wyneken, gave a classic response: "We will not tolerate it that the souls freed and purchased by the blood of Christ be brought again under the yoke of any little Lutheran pope. . . . The dignity, the desire, and the joy of the true co-worker of God is to draw ever more his community of believers into their freedom and its worthy use, to encourage them and lead them ever more in the exercise of their rights, to show them how to exercise their duties that they be more and more convinced of their high calling and that they demonstrate that they are ever more worthy of that calling." In so elevating the dignity of the vocations of the laity, says Wyneken, the people love and honor the Office of the Ministry all the more.

A Sacred Vocation

I recently had the opportunity to visit the Lutheran Church of Australia. (I studied in Adelaide on exchange in 1987, and I've enjoyed the friendships of many Australian Lutherans ever since.) Dr. Andrew Pfeiffer, head of the school with a PhD in missiology, invited me into his office at the seminary. He pointed to a shelf full of books, and in his delightful Australian manner and accent, said, "See all those books? Those are all the mission gimmicks and programs that were supposed to save the Lutheran Church of Australia. None of them worked. Not a one."

Andrew's been teaching his seminary students something very simple but profoundly important: Pastors are to teach the Lutheran view of vocation for laity. Each of us has a divine calling, a vocation. In fact, that vocation is multifaceted. Our vocations place us in contexts where we serve God through our neighbors.

Luther was a master of the Bible's teaching on vocation and wrote eloquently and very simply about the high callings of everyday life, like those of mother, father, sister, brother, grandparent, worker, butcher, baker or farmer. He rightly pointed out that the calling of mother is every bit as holy and divinely pleasing as that of pastor! "Whatsoever you have done to the least of these, you've done to Me" applies to diapers. (And Luther, by the way, expected fathers to change them too!) Forgiven in Christ, Christians are freed to serve those around them according to the station in life they occupy.

Dr. Pfeiffer teaches that, in the context of our vocations and especially as we interact with relatives, friends and neighbors, we share Christ and His Gospel of free forgiveness while inviting folks to church. Pfeiffer is teaching his students the importance of conducting regular membership classes and encouraging and training his people to invite others. It's simple but vital for the salvation of souls and the mission of the Church.

The Church needs clergy and laity in the mission field as called professionals. But just as profound is the vocation each of us has where we are to speak Christ and invite people to church. Each of us is a saint, a spiritual priest, who offers sacrifices of prayer ("Pray the Lord of the harvest send workers"), praise and thanksgiving. Each of us can and must support the Church's work of global mission and sending missionaries, a sacrifice of praise

(2 Corinthians 9:6–15). Each of us in our relationships has a sacred vocation, however humbly, to speak of Christ to our loved ones and neighbors and speak forgiveness in His name!

Prayer

A Simple Way to Pray

After about a year and a half in this position, I've discovered that, if nothing else, being Synod president does tend to improve one's prayer life. A prayer Luther often prayed at night says it all: "My dear God, now I lie down and turn Your affairs back to You; You may do better with them. If You can do no better than I, You will ruin them entirely. When I awake, I will gladly try again."

Because of a feisty barber named Peter Beskendorf, we not only know exactly how Martin Luther prayed, but we have what is probably the greatest and most practical little pamphlet ever written on how regular folks can pray: *A Simple Way to Pray"* (CPH, 2012). While Luther was getting lathered in the barber's chair, Peter asked the Reformer how he went about praying. Luther gave Peter the lowdown in the chair and then sat down and peeled off his little book shortly thereafter. Because there are so many unbiblical things said and written about prayer all about us, every Lutheran should have *A Simple Way to Pray* and read it. *Luther's little book on prayer will revolutionize your prayer life.*

The genius of Luther's approach is that it anchors prayer in the biblical or biblically based text so that it doesn't float off into self-absorbed drivel, quite disconnected from God's mandates and promises in the Bible. Luther's approach balances the issue of order and freedom, written prayer and *ex corde* prayer—but in such a way that the biblical text determines the content and inspires the mind to pray freely as the Spirit moves.

Luther followed a simple, fourfold pattern:

1. INSTRUCTION

2. THANKSGIVING

3. CONFESSION

4. PRAYER

I call it "I.T.C.P." This is how Luther "prayed" the Small Catechism—something I'd long heard about but had not the slightest idea what it meant. Virtually any text of the Bible can be prayed this way, or for that matter, any biblically based prayer.

It's Lent. I invite you to pray daily with me the greatest prayer ever written (aside from those in the Bible): The Litany (*LSB*, pp. 288–89). This 1,500-year-old prayer, which Luther loved, covers the extent of real spiritual and physical need for the Church and the world. And it's all right out of the Bible. When you come to the following text, let Luther's I.T.C.P. mode kick in. Here's an example: *We poor sinners implore You . . . to preserve all pastors and ministers of Your Church in the true knowledge and understanding of Your wholesome Word and to sustain them in holy living.*

Lord, You INSTRUCT us that it is Your deepest desire that pastors love and stick to Your Word, for themselves and for others. It's horrible when a pastor forsakes the Word and falls into error or gross sin and does untold damage in the Church. We also know that it is Your deepest desire, Lord, that we pray for our pastors.

Lord, I give You THANKS for my pastor and all pastors of the Church. In this crazy day and age, it's a miracle that I have a pastor who believes the Bible, preaches Law and Gospel, loves his people and serves me and my family.

Lord, I CONFESS that I fail to pray for my pastor. I don't even think about our seminaries until we have a vacancy. I've been stingy in supporting my pastor. I have not always put the best construction on his actions and have failed to follow Matthew 18 when I've had a concern. I have disregarded the fact that You have placed this man to dole out your previous gifts of the Gospel to me.

Lord, I PRAY, enlighten me by Your Word and Spirit. Be with my pastor, and strengthen him today. Cause him to love Your "wholesome Word." Protect him and his wife and family from the evil one. "Sustain him in holy living," and give him joy in his vocation. Cause me to be a source of joy in his ministry, and give me a generous heart that I may support the ministry of the Gospel in this place in every way. Amen.

Blessed Lent.

Be Bold in Your Prayers

Rev. Dr. John Kleinig, an old friend from Australia, recently gave a marvelous presentation at a Doxology retreat. Doxology (*www.doxology.us/*) is an organization that assists pastors in the craft of caring for themselves, their families and their congregations. After a wild and woolly year of service, I thought it would be healthy for the president's staff to attend a retreat along with roughly 170 pastors and their spouses. It was so refreshing.

One presentation particularly struck me. Dr. Kleinig lectured on "Access to the Father's Grace: Finding Help for Ourselves and Others." As Christians, we have a sacred and priestly calling (Hebrews 3:1). In the Old Testament, access to God's saving presence was strictly limited. Once a year, after thorough ritual washing, the high priest entered the Holy of Holies, the innermost sanctum of the temple, carrying blood for the sin offering. The blood was sprinkled liberally about the mercy seat, the ark of the covenant and the altar.

Jesus has rendered us all spiritual priests with access to the Father's saving presence in His blessed Word and Sacrament. "Therefore my brothers, since we have confidence for entry into the sanctuary by the blood of Jesus, by the new and living way that he inaugurated for us through the curtain, that is, through his flesh, and since we have a great high priest over the house of God, let us come near with a true heart in full assurance of faith, with our hearts sprinkled from an evil conscience and our bodies washed with pure water" (Hebrews 10:19–22).

The apostolic writer is telling us that in Holy Baptism we are freed from sin and given a clean conscience. Our hearts are purified by forgiveness in the Sacrament of the Altar, and we have access—unhindered and rendered holy by Jesus—to stand in the holy presence of God Almighty. In fact, Jesus is our High Priest, interceding with the Father on our behalf. In Jesus, we know we have not only access to the Father but also the Father's willing and ready approval!

What does this mean for us priests? Many things, but especially that we can approach God with boldness in our prayers (Hebrews 4:14, 16). There are many verses in the New Testament where people bring others to Jesus for help (Matthew 4:24; 8:16; 9:2, 32;

12:22; 14:35; 15:30; 17:17; 19:13), and we can do that same thing through our prayers. Think of the paralytic let down through the roof. The healing of this man was done by Jesus because of the faith of his friends. ("And when Jesus saw their faith . . ." [Mark 2:5].) What a marvelous text for us spiritual priests!

Dr. Kleinig shared with us his own practice of writing down the names of a half-dozen individuals whose situations had come to his attention the previous week. During the service, the Prayer of the Church and Holy Communion, he prays for them. In the ancient church, the people who were prayed for weekly in the service were listed in the diptych, a sort of hinged tablet. In addition to my daily morning prayer—where I pray for an ever-changing and growing list of people and churches—I'm taking my personal diptych to church this Sunday.

We can be as bold and confident of the Lord's concern and compassion for our needy loved one, unbaptized grandchild or wayward brother as those men who were so bold as to remove the roof tiles and lower their friend right in front of Jesus' face. In fact, Jesus loves to have us do this. He delights in our supplication and is humbled to bring our needs before the Father. This is our great privilege as priests. We have access right into the Holy of Holies, and through prayer, we can even bring friends into God's presence. Be bold in your prayers for your friends and loved ones. Tear out the roof!

Hope and Joy

Prisoners of Advent Hope

The prophet Zechariah lived after the great Babylonian Captivity and encouraged the people of God, pointing to the Christ to come. He also gave us one of our great Advent texts about the coming Christ.

> Rejoice greatly, O daughter of Zion!
> Shout aloud, O daughter of Jerusalem!
> Behold, your king is coming to you;
> righteous and having salvation is he,
> humble and mounted on a donkey,
> on a colt, the foal of a donkey. (Zechariah 9:9)

Advent means "coming." In these weeks of December, we are humbled by the Law with themes of repentance. "Repent! For the kingdom of God is at hand!"—the first sermon out of John the Baptizer's mouth and that of Jesus (Matthew 3:2; 4:17). We are reminded that Christ came as a babe in Bethlehem, born as God and man to go from cradle to cross. Christ continues to come to us in His blessed Word (Romans 10:17) and in absolution (John 20:21f.), Baptism (Galatians 3:27) and the Supper (1 Corinthians 10:16–17). And Christ will come again at the resurrection. "I will come again and take you to myself" (John 14:3). Thus, Advent looks to the past, the present and to the future with hope!

Another line from Zechariah strikes me: "Return to your stronghold, *O prisoners of hope*; today I declare that I will restore to you double" (Zechariah 9:12). Because this world is closer to its end, this word of hope is more precious today than it was in 520 BC. Despite this wretched world, the economic malaise, the political nonsense, the global conflict, the ubiquitous threat of Islam, the decline of the Church in the West, the shocking reality that our government now calls evil what the Bible calls good and calls good what the Bible calls evil, despite it all, I remain a "prisoner of hope." I am chained to an ultimate, optimistic future! I am captive to the hope of Christ.

The Bible said it would be so. "The Gentiles will hope in his [Christ's!] name" (Matthew 12:21). Christians are people of hope. Hope is rooted deep in the ancient promises of the Old Testament. Hope fills the Psalms (e.g., Psalms 130:7; 119:49), which time and again refer us to the mighty deeds of the Lord as anchors for the steadfast truth of His promises, come what may.

The New Testament explodes in hopefulness. Through Christ, we have "access by faith into this grace," and so "we rejoice in the hope of the glory of God" (Romans 5:2). Trials produce endurance, character and hope, "and hope does not put us to shame" (Romans 5:4–5). Yes, the whole creation creaks and cracks under the burden of sin, but it is all for a hopeful purpose (Romans 8:8). Faith is certainty in Christ's promises, though unseen, and thus faith is also hope, and that means hope brings patience (Romans 8:24–25). Because we know the end of the story and its certain, resurrected life with Christ, "through the encouragement of the Scriptures, we . . . have hope" (Romans 15:4).

Are you hopeless? Bury yourself in the Scriptures! Paul reminded the Romans that the Scriptures promised that "the root of Jesse will come. . . . In him the Gentiles will hope!" (Romans 15:12). And this blessing is as powerful today as when Paul wrote it: "May the God of hope fill you with all joy and peace in believing, so that by the power of the Holy Spirit you may abound in hope" (Romans 15:13).

We know that eternity is ours; we have nothing but eternal life ahead. Each of us has a vocation, a calling, and a Christian calling at that—a special purpose assigned us by God in this life to serve and love those around us. Peter gives us a mandate to speak of Christ in our vocations: "But in your hearts honor Christ the Lord as holy, always being prepared to make a defense to anyone who asks you for a reason for the hope that is in you; yet do it with gentleness and respect" (1 Peter 3:15). You have Christ for you, and "Christ in you, the hope of glory" (Colossians 1:27).

So, don't "grieve as others do who have no hope" (1 Thessalonians 4:13), as you face death and trials of this life. This Advent, come what may, "Let us hold fast the confession of our hope without wavering, for he who promised is faithful" (Hebrews 10:23).

O Lord, at Thy coming, make us, keep us, find us "prisoners of hope."

Works of God

I'll never forget my first visit to Bethesda Lutheran Communities in Watertown, Wisconsin. As we walked along, we had the opportunity to greet and observe a number of individuals with profound disabilities. One man, I recall, used an electronic device with a keyboard to communicate with us. He was busy about his job stripping copper wire from an unusable electrical motor. He had his vocation. Slowly and methodically, he produced a large pile of copper to be recycled. I was fascinated to learn that many such individuals actually bid for various jobs and enjoy compensation for their work. While Bethesda provides group care for a number of people with disabilities, its goal was and is to have those with disabilities do for themselves and become active, integral members of the body of Christ—the Church on earth.

As biblical Christians, we treasure all life—in whatever way God chooses to provide it. There is a continuity in our views regarding drugs that kill life in the womb; government programs that force us to pay for such drugs; the value of children, no matter what their context or genetic makeup; and the value of every life from conception to grave and in a resurrected eternity. There is simply no other option for those who believe what Jesus told Nicodemus, "For God so loved the world that he gave his only begotten Son."

Today, the wonderful thing about work with those with disabilities is that these people are more and more respected for their particular gifts and are encouraged to find and flourish in their particular vocations as they serve in and among us as the Church. While those who are hearing impaired or unable to see face specific challenges in life, these individuals—often knowing no other state of existence—don't view their disabilities as disabilities at all. In fact, their challenges in life have helped to give them, and all of us, a unique perspective on living life that is rich in our Lord's grace.

Some years ago, while traveling in the Baltics, I first became aware of the worldwide challenges many who have disabilities face. At that time in Latvia, as in the former Soviet Union and in virtually the whole developing world, those with disabilities (mental or physical) were most often shunted out of sight. People with disabilities bore the burden that a larger society imposed upon them because very often society associated disability with divine retribution. When seeing a man blind from birth, Jesus' disciples asked him, "Rabbi, who sinned, this man or his parents, that he was born blind?" Jesus answered, "It was not that this man sinned, or his parents, but that the works of God might be displayed in him" (John 9:2–3). In our congregations today, there are still a myriad of opportunities for us to behold the "works of God" made manifest among us in and with people who have disabilities.

There are great ministries of mercy and outreach happening right now through individuals who themselves are challenged. Unfortunately, disabled populations are hugely unchurched. Opportunities abound for a vibrant ministry of mercy and life together with families and parents who care for profoundly impaired children.

About Joy

Several years ago—at the advice of a dear friend—I took a hard look at what might seem for me a rather unlikely topic: joy in the Christian life. "So many pastors and Christians have so little joy today," my friend observed. "These are difficult times."

At first, I scoffed at the prospect. Isn't joy a topic reserved for the slick TV preachers? Isn't it the domain of the "prosperity preachers" who get virtually every chief part of the Small Catechism wrong? Isn't joy more the mere foam on the beer rather than the tasty draught itself? But against my dour and better judgment, I determined, with a decided grimace, to open a Bible.

Soon I was racing through the pages, text to text to text. My memory was bolstered by concordances and commentaries piled about my Christmas vacation easy chair. I was dumbfounded to find the topic of joy shot through the Bible. I found joy and rejoicing pervading the Psalms (4, 5, 16, 30, 51). I found joy in the Prophets (Isaiah 35) and in the Gospels (John 15–16). I found joy on the lips of Jesus (Luke 10:20) and in the lives of the people He touched (Luke 2:10). I found joy on the lips of Mary (Luke 1:47) and Zechariah (Luke 2:67ff.), in the womb of Elizabeth (Luke 2:41ff.), on the lips of angels (Luke 2:10). I found joy at the manger. I found joy at the resurrection (Luke 24:41). I found joy over life (Ecclesiastes 9), joy in the midst of death (John 11:14–15), joy in worship (Psalm 100). I found joy amidst persecution and suffering (Luke 6:23; Colossians 1:24). I found Paul's letters packed with joy (Galatians 5:22). There is even joy in repentance (Psalm 51:8). I found joy in references to faith and hope and love. I found joy over the gifts of friends, work, family, food, children and marriage. I found joy over new believers! And more important than anything else, I found reference after reference to the Lord's joy over me, sinner that I am (Luke 15:20–24). And guess what? I began to rejoice over it all!

If you, dear reader, are anything like me, you recoil at the tiniest whiff of compulsion, of a forced and coerced approach to joy. For Pete's sake, if I lack joy—and we all do in one way or another—someone telling me to be more joyful is about as joy-inducing as a dental drill! Inspecting the Word of God on the topic, however, is quite a different matter. You see, the mighty and active Word of God actually delivers what it talks about. Its Law actually damns

(Jeremiah 23:29). Its forgiving Gospel actually forgives in the reading and hearing and preaching of it. "For the Word of God is living and active, sharper than any two-edged sword, piercing to the division of soul and spirit" (Hebrews 4:12). And the very Word of God can create and sustain a joy the likes of which we've barely conceived. That's why it's vital for this life that we let the Word of God have its way with us, that we "buy while the market is open."

In the Bible, joy is much like faith itself. It flickers and wavers. At times, it appears to be snuffed out altogether. And yet through every storm and trial, the very things that threaten it actually kindle it and bring it to a blaze. Joy may be a simple smile at the blessing of another sunrise, a profound happiness at a family reconciled or a belly sore from laughing over an evening with old friends. As joy is tested and grows, we even learn to "rejoice in our sufferings," because we know they produce great things in our lives.

The Lord has created us for joy and has provided His Word to give it to us no matter what we face. "Rejoice in the Lord always; again I will say, rejoice!" (Philippians 4:4).

Resurrection

Death's Precarious Toehold

In a beautiful treatment of the resurrection of Christ, Luther compares the resurrection to a birth:

> Christ, our head, has arisen. But now that the Head is seated on high and lives, there is no longer any reason for concern. We who cling to Him must also follow after Him as His body and members. For where the head goes and abides, there the body with all the members must necessarily follow and abide. As in the birth of man and of all animals, the head naturally appears first, and after this is born, the whole body follows easily. Now since Christ has passed over and reigns above in heaven over sin, death, devil, and everything, and since He did this for our sake to draw us after Him, we need no longer worry about our resurrection and life, though we depart and rot in the ground. For now this is no more than a sleep. And for Christ it is but a night before He rouses us from the sleep. (Luther's Works, vol. 28, p. 110, *Commentary on 1 Corinthians 15*)

The hard part is done. The walls of the fortress of death, sadness and gloom have been breached—yes, razed at the foundation! Says Luther, because of Christ's resurrection, "all the hold death still has on us is by a small toe!" In Baptism, we've been united with Christ. So we shall go where He goes. Through cross, trial and into death? Yes . . . but with Christ through death to life and resurrection (Romans 6:1ff.).

That's the secret to a joyous life, come what may. Read the Book of Acts, and you will quickly find that the powerful evangelistic preaching of the apostles was very simple. This Jesus is the Christ, foretold by the prophets (Acts 2:25ff.). "You crucified and killed [him] by the hands of lawless men" (Acts 2:23). "God raised him up, loosing the pangs of death, because it was not possible for him to be held by it" (Acts 2:24).

It was a straightforward message of (1) prophecy fulfilled; (2) stinging Law directed full force, right between the eyes; and (3) sweetest Gospel. Believe and be baptized for the forgiveness of your sins. By faith, all that is Christ's is yours. In Baptism, you are connected with Him, and both His death for sin and resurrection to life are yours. We depart from this type of evangelistic preaching (Scripture/Law/Gospel/Resurrection/Baptism) at our own eternal peril, to the detriment of the Church.

Too simple? Hardly. It's God's apostolic outline for preaching—for reaching the lost and forgiving and empowering the baptized (however creatively applied!). And note how utterly objective it is! Notice who the actor is! God promised this Christ in the Scriptures! God's Law damns you! God's Gospel of the resurrection—of Christ put to death for our transgressions and raised for our justification (Romans 4:25)—forgives you! The hard part is done! "It is finished" (John 19:30). Believe it, and it's yours! There is *nothing* to do. Only receive! Joy!

This is the resurrection source of the apostles' joy—a joy that would not whither, even under the whip (death's toehold). "They beat them and charged them not to speak in the name of Jesus, and let them go. Then they [the apostles] left . . . rejoicing that they were counted worthy to suffer dishonor for the name" (Acts 2:41). "Reconciled by his death," "saved by his life," "we rejoice in God!" (Romans 5:9ff.). Trials (pinched toes) push us to repentance, which is the path to joy (Psalm 51). And so the apostles and prophets bid us rejoice in trials (1 Peter 1:3–6). They point us to Jesus in every tribulation, all purposefully sent by God for our good (Romans 8:37ff.), "who for the joy set before him, endured the cross" (Hebrews 12:1–2). The apostles invite the baptized to "suffer together" and "rejoice together" (1 Corinthians 12:26) for a more fulsome joy!

The very resurrection of Christ—come home to us in Baptism (Colossians 2:12)—frees us to breach the walls of pride and hatred and envy. We are freed to not expect those around us to be anything but sinners in need of Law/Gospel and love, just like we are (1 Timothy 1:15)! We are freed to rejoice in family and friends. We are freed to face death, even death, with the resurrection resolve that has grabbed hold of us in Christ. He's been through it all. He knows the way. He is the way.

Sin, death and the devil still pinch toes. They've got a toehold to be sure . . . but only a toehold! And not for long.

Blessed Easter!

Photo Credits

Introduction
Rev. Dr. Matthew C. Harrison, president of The Lutheran Church—Missouri Synod, preaches during the Festival Dedication Service at the Town and Parish Church of St. Mary's before the dedication of The International Lutheran Center at the Old Latin School on Sunday, May 3, 2015, in Wittenberg, Germany. LCMS Communications/Erik M. Lunsford. Copyright © 2015 The Lutheran Church—Missouri Synod.

Repentance
Rev. Eric Andrae absolves a participant in St. Francis Xavier College Church during the 2015 TABOO National LCMS Campus Ministry Conference on Tuesday, January 6, 2015, at St. Louis University in St. Louis. LCMS Communications/Erik M. Lunsford. Copyright © 2015 The Lutheran Church—Missouri Synod.

Forgiveness
Rev. Tim Droegemueller, senior pastor, blesses a child during distribution of the Sacrament at Divine Service on Sunday, November 23, 2014, at Living Faith Lutheran Church in Cumming, Georgia. LCMS Communications/Erik M. Lunsford. Copyright © 2014 The Lutheran Church—Missouri Synod.

The Bible
A young student watches a film about Jesus following worship on Sunday, April 12, 2015, at Mount Calvary Lutheran Church in Holdrege, Nebraska. LCMS Communications/Erik M. Lunsford. Copyright © 2015 The Lutheran Church—Missouri Synod.

The Church
Rev. Matthew Clark baptizes 21 Nepali immigrants, including Ran Gurung, on Sunday, January 12, 2014, at Ascension Lutheran Church in St. Louis. LCMS Communications/Erik M. Lunsford. Copyright © 2014 The Lutheran Church—Missouri Synod/Erik M. Lunsford.

Congregational Life
Rev. Ulmer Marshall greets Valarie Floyd-Bridges following worship at Trinity Lutheran Church on Sunday, April 6, 2014, in Mobile, Alabama. LCMS Communications/Erik M. Lunsford. Copyright © 2014 The Lutheran Church—Missouri Synod.

Witness and Mission

Vicar David Blas, missionary-at-large at LCMS Sheboygan County Hispanic Outreach and St. John's Lutheran Church of Plymouth, Wisconsin, witnesses at La Conquistadora, a Mexican grocery store, on Thursday, January 28, 2016, in Sheboygan, Wisconsin. Blas also handed out *Portals of Prayer* booklets and dropped off Bibles. LCMS Communications/Erik M. Lunsford. Copyright © 2016 The Lutheran Church—Missouri Synod.

Church and State

Photographs from the 2015 March for Life on Thursday, January 22, 2015, in Washington DC. LCMS Communications/Erik M. Lunsford. Copyright © 2015 The Lutheran Church—Missouri Synod.

Family and Vocation

Rev. Wally Arp, senior pastor of St. Luke's Lutheran Church, marries Toni and Craig Vining at the church on Saturday, March 5, 2016, in Oviedo, Florida. LCMS Communications/Erik M. Lunsford. Copyright © 2016 The Lutheran Church—Missouri Synod.

Prayer

Alexa Obermier prays during worship on Sunday, April 12, 2015, at Mount Calvary Lutheran Church in Holdrege, Nebraska. LCMS Communications/Erik M. Lunsford. Copyright © 2015 The Lutheran Church—Missouri Synod.

Hope and Joy

A young student listens as Rev. Herb Burch, LCMS career missionary to Peru (not pictured), entertains the class with a song about Jesus at the Noe school, one of many places affected by recent landslides near Lima, Peru, on Tuesday, April 7, 2015. LCMS Communications/Erik M. Lunsford. Copyright © 2015 The Lutheran Church—Missouri Synod.

Resurrection

Interior photograph of Chapel of Christ Triumphant at Concordia University Wisconsin in Mequon, Wisconsin, on Wednesday, May 28, 2014. LCMS Communications/Erik M. Lunsford. Copyright © 2014 The Lutheran Church—Missouri Synod.

Scripture Index